Thomas Dunbar Ingram

A History of the Legislative Union of Great Britain and Ireland

Thomas Dunbar Ingram

A History of the Legislative Union of Great Britain and Ireland

ISBN/EAN: 9783744717151

Printed in Europe, USA, Canada, Australia, Japan

Cover: Foto ©ninafisch / pixelio.de

More available books at **www.hansebooks.com**

A HISTORY OF

THE LEGISLATIVE UNION

OF

GREAT BRITAIN AND IRELAND

BY

T. DUNBAR INGRAM, LL.D.,

OF LINCOLN'S INN, BARRISTER-AT-LAW; FORMERLY PROFESSOR OF JURISPRUDENCE AND OF
HINDOO AND MUHAMMEDAN LAW IN THE PRESIDENCY COLLEGE, CALCUTTA.

"We are therefore, I conceive, entitled to cast aside as an utter calumny, the allegation of bribery against the members of the Scottish Parliament. Exactly the same allegation, and on just as flimsy grounds, was, on occasion of the Irish Union a century afterwards, brought against the members of the Irish Parliament."

LORD STANHOPE, *Reign of Queen Anne.*

London:
MACMILLAN AND CO.
AND NEW YORK
1887

The right of translation is reserved.

PREFACE.

THOUGH a century has not elapsed since the Legislative Union of Great Britain and Ireland was accomplished, ignorance or doubt has gathered round its history. Misrepresentation and unworthy declamation have obscured all the facts of the case. The original sources of information have been neglected or wilfully avoided, and credit has been given to statements in one-sided and extravagant books, like *Grattan's Life*,[1] or worthless publications such as Barrington's romances. Of these writings, it is not too much to say that, in them almost every event which occurred during the progress of the Union contest, is misrepresented, exaggerated, or coloured

---

[1] One assertion of the younger Grattan will show us the value of his statements. He says "Only 7,000 individuals petitioned in favour of the Union, and 110,000 freeholders and 707,000 persons signed petitions against the measure." He gives no authority for this statement. Of the seventy-four declarations and petitions in favour of the Union, four alone, those sent forward by the Catholics of Wexford city, of county Leitrim and of county Roscommon, and the mixed declaration of county Tyrone, were signed by upwards of 9,330 persons.

to suit the opinions of their authors, and that everything favourable to the Government is carefully kept out of sight.

Dissatisfied with endless assertions unaccompanied by proof, the author of the present work determined to investigate the subject for himself. For this purpose he examined closely and in detail the original and contemporaneous authorities. At an early stage of the inquiry he was surprised to find that there was no evidence to sustain the accusations made against the manner in which the Union was carried, and that all the charges against the Government rested finally on the stories of Barrington, or on the declamatory statements of the Opposition during the sessions of 1799 and 1800, statements which, when the anti-Unionists were challenged in both Houses of Parliament to substantiate, they declined to do so. As the author proceeded in his search, he discovered that, after its terms were made known, and the public had had time for reflection, the Union was thankfully accepted by the two communities which made up Ireland; that the Protestants, after the first burst of clamour, were, as a body, converted, and became well-wishers to the measure; and that the Catholics, after a short hesitation, gave the Union their hearty assent and support.

The whole inquiry has left a strong conviction on the

author's mind that the Union was undertaken from the purest motives, that it was carried by fair and constitutional means, and that its final accomplishment was accompanied with the hearty assent and concurrence of the vast majority of the two peoples that dwelt in Ireland. And he now lays before the public the evidence which has produced that conviction, supporting every statement of fact by reference to his authorities.

Though, in the writer's opinion, the Irish Union is free from any taint of corruption, yet a grave mistake was committed at its close, in that it was not immediately followed up by its natural complement, the emancipation of the Catholics not only in Ireland, but also throughout the Empire. This was not, however, the fault of the three eminent statesmen who carried the measure—Pitt, Cornwallis, and Castlereagh.

DUBLIN,
April 15, 1887.

CONTENTS.

CHAPTER I.

EARLY LEGISLATIVE CONNECTIONS BETWEEN ENGLAND AND IRELAND.—POYNINGS' LAW. — ATTEMPTS OF THE IRISH PARLIAMENT AT A LEGISLATIVE UNION.—THE PENAL CODE.—OPINIONS OF DISTINGUISHED WRITERS AND THINKERS ON THE ADVANTAGES OF A LEGISLATIVE UNION 1

CHAPTER II.

STATE OF THE REPRESENTATION OF IRELAND BETWEEN 1793 AND 1800.—COMPARED WITH THAT OF ENGLAND—WITH THAT OF SCOTLAND. 21

CHAPTER III.

NATURE OF THE CONNECTION WHICH EXISTED BETWEEN GREAT BRITAIN AND IRELAND AFTER 1782.—ITS DANGERS.—TENDENCIES TO SEPARATION AS SHOWN BY THE REFUSAL OF A COMMERCIAL TREATY—THE REGENCY QUESTION—ACTUAL AND PROPOSED IRISH LEGISLATION. 45

CHAPTER IV.

UNION DEBATES IN THE IRISH PARLIAMENT, 1799. 83

CONTENTS.

CHAPTER V.

SENTIMENTS OF THE PROTESTANT COMMUNITY ON A UNION.—THE MEASURE AT FIRST DISAPPROVED OF.—CHANGE OF OPINION IN ITS FAVOUR.—DECLARATIONS AND PETITIONS FOR AND AGAINST IT.—BRIBERY BY THE OPPOSITION.—ATTEMPTS OF THE ANTI-UNIONISTS TO EXCITE THE COUNTRY AGAINST THE UNION. . . . 107

CHAPTER VI.

SENTIMENTS OF THE CATHOLIC COMMUNITY ON THE UNION.—SUPPORT GIVEN TO THAT MEASURE—BY THEIR PEERAGE—THEIR HIERARCHY—THEIR INFERIOR CLERGY—THEIR LAITY. 139

CHAPTER VII.

UNION DEBATES IN THE IRISH PARLIAMENT, 1800. 163

CHAPTER VIII.

ACCUSATIONS AGAINST THE GOVERNMENT.—COMPENSATION TO THE PROPRIETORS OF BOROUGHS. — BESTOWAL OF PEERAGES. — ALLEGED INTERFERENCE WITH THE RIGHT OF PETITIONING.—DISMISSAL OF GOVERNMENT OFFICIALS. 178

CHAPTER IX.

ACCUSATIONS AGAINST THE GOVERNMENT, *continued*.—MONEY PAYMENTS TO MEMBERS FOR THEIR VOTES.—MILITARY TERRORISM. . 206

A HISTORY OF

THE LEGISLATIVE UNION

OF

GREAT BRITAIN AND IRELAND.

A HISTORY OF
THE LEGISLATIVE UNION
OF
GREAT BRITAIN AND IRELAND.

CHAPTER I.

Early legislative connections between England and Ireland.—Poynings' Law.—Attempts of the Irish Parliament at a Legislative Union.—The Penal Code.—Opinions of distinguished writers and thinkers on the advantages of a Legislative Union.

IN the reign of Edward I. barons, prelates, and citizens were summoned from Ireland to serve in the English Parliament, and did serve therein. We find in the White Book of the Exchequer in Dublin a writ issued in the ninth year of this king to his Chancellor of Ireland, wherein are mentioned " Quædam statuta per nos de assensu Prelatorum, Comitum, Baronum et communitates regni nostri Hiberniæ nuper apud Lincoln et quædam alia statuta postmodum apud Eborum facta."[1]

Prynne discovered a writ whereby in the eighth year of Edward II. Lords of Ireland were summoned to a

[1] Molyneux, *Case of Ireland*, 95.

Parliament at Westminster to treat and confer " de aliis negotiis arduis et urgentibus nos contingentibus." But he denied that this was a summons to them as members of the Parliament, on the ground that the words " vestrumque consilium impensuri " were wanting in the writ. Leland points out that these words were not at the time a necessary part of it, several subsequent and undoubted writs not containing them.[1] Prynne also overlooked a prior writ of the second year of this king directed to " R. electo Dublin episcopo cæterisque Episcopis necnon Abbatibus et Prioribus."[2]

In the reign of Edward III. Irish representatives served in the English Parliament. We find in the fiftieth year of this king a writ directed to the Lord Justice of Ireland and the Archbishop of Dublin, requiring them to issue writs to the several counties, cities, and boroughs " for satisfying the expenses of the men of that land who last came over to serve in Parliament in England."[3] In another roll of the same year, the case of John Draper, who served in the English Parliament for Cork, is mentioned.[4]

In this year also writs were again issued to Irish constituencies to send members to the Parliament at Westminster, and we have the returns made to them by the clergy, cities, and boroughs. In the majority of these returns, though not in all, the electors declare that they are not bound to send representatives to the English Parliament. Notwithstanding, they go on to say, on account of their reverence for the king and his present

---

[1] Leland, vol. ii. App.
[2] *Ib.* and Dugdale, 65.
[3] Molyneux, 97.
[4] *Ib.*

necessity, they have elected persons to repair to Westminster, and to treat and consult with him and his Council.[1]

Owing principally to the danger and difficulty of the journey, the practice of sending representatives to the English Parliament from Ireland was given up, and the regular course of Irish Parliaments established.[2]

Voyages between England and Ireland were not formerly frequent, and many things happened in the latter kingdom which were not known till long afterwards in England. The Irish Viceroy, or Deputy, had, before the reign of Henry VII., the power of giving the royal assent to Irish bills without their being considered in England by the king and his council. Though at times a specific prohibition was conveyed to a Viceroy against passing any laws which had not been examined in England, there was no general enactment on the subject. This system occasionally gave rise to a difference of policy between the two countries, which was agreeable neither to the English Government nor to the Anglo-Irish colony. In the reign of Henry VII. a successful attempt was made by the Irish Parliament to connect itself more closely with the Government in England. This was effected by the enactment known as Poynings' law, so often misrepresented or misunderstood. This statute provided that all laws intended to be passed in

---

[1] Leland, vol. i. App. In one of the Union debates Sir Laurence Parsons said that it was the Irish Parliament which protested against Irish representatives being summoned to England. It was really some of the *constituencies* which protested.

[2] Molyneux, 98.   [3] *Parl. Deb.* i. 154.

Ireland should be certified under the great seal of that kingdom, as a mark of authority that they really came from the Irish Parliament, and that they should be returned by the king under his great seal, as a warrant authorising the Irish Governor to give the royal assent to them. The Anglo-Irish had long suffered from the folly or injustice of the local government, which was able to model the Parliament, dictate laws, and impose taxes at its will. The treason of a Deputy had frequently drawn general and severe punishment on the subjects of the pale. Ireland was at this time intensely Yorkist, and the White Rose had firmly maintained itself in that country for nine years after the battle of Bosworth.[1] Shortly before the passing of Poynings' law Lambert Simnel had been crowned king at Christ's Church, in Dublin, with the connivance of the Deputy, Kildare. A Parliament had been convened, in which laws were passed, taxes imposed, and vengeance denounced against those who should oppose the pretender.[2] It was to protect the king on the one side, and the Irish subjects on the other, that Poynings' law was passed. This enactment was made, in its own words, "at the request of the Commons of that land." Far from being considered as a restriction, it was looked upon as a safeguard, and no Act was ever more popular.[3]

[1] In the reign of Henry VI. the Duke of York had been for ten years Viceroy in Ireland, and had planted many of his adherents there.—Flood, *Parl. Deb.* i. 151.   [2] Leland, ii. 8.

[3] "Do we understand its meaning better than the people in whose days it was passed, or they who succeeded for an hundred years after? By them it was considered as a boon and a favour." —Flood, *Parl. Deb.* i. 152.

The Irish Parliament and public long considered this law as the best security of the subject. During the reign of Elizabeth the Irish Government repeatedly contended for its occasional suspension. With one exception, the people vigorously and successfully opposed these attempts.[1] Dublin was then practically as distant from London as America now is. The little and distant colony of Englishmen dreaded the unauthorised power of a Lord Deputy, supported by a Parliament composed of his own creatures. Poynings' Act was really intended to prevent the Irish Deputies from passing laws through interested motives or under frivolous pretences, and giving them the royal assent without the knowledge of the sovereign.[2]

During the Commonwealth Ireland was incorporated with the rest of the empire, and sent thirty representatives to the Protectorate Parliaments of 1654 and 1657 respectively.[3] After the Restoration this system ceased, and things returned to the old state of separate legislatures.

In 1703 the Irish Parliament made an attempt at an incorporate or legislative union with England, which, unfortunately, was not successful. Mr. Froude has told us the story of this attempt. "On the 29th of

---

[1] Leland, vol. ii. App. Flood, *Parl. Deb.* i. 152.
[2] *Grattan's Life*, i. 94.
[3] The new Great Seal ordered by the Long Parliament and used by Cromwell, had on one side the arms of England and Ireland with the inscription, "The Great Seal of England;" on the other a representation of the House of Commons sitting within the motto, "In the first year of freedom by God's blessing restored."— Clarendon's *Hist.*

September the Commons voted an address to the Queen protesting against the suspicion that they wished to make Ireland independent, and declaring their entire conviction that their welfare depended on the maintenance of the connection with England. On the 4th of October Southwell wrote that the Commons had sat that day to consider the state of the nation, and after some hours' sitting and considering the many misfortunes the country lay under, all the speakers concluded that they did in most earnest manner desire a union with England." "On the 20th of October they framed their most serious discontents and desires into a direct address to the Crown. After enumerating their distresses they implored the Queen to concede the only means which could remove them—a firm and strict union with England."[1]

On October 25th in the same year, the Irish House of Lords, having taken into their serious consideration the state of the nation, came to the following resolution :— "That it was their opinion upon due consideration of the present constitution of this kingdom that such an humble representation be made to the Queen of the state and condition thereof as may best incline Her Majesty, by such proper means as to Her Majesty should seem fit, to promote such an union with England as may qualify the states of this kingdom to be represented there."[2]

In 1707 the Irish Commons again returned to this matter. In their address of congratulation to the

[1] *English in Ireland*, 300-301.
[2] *House of Lords Journals*, ii. 29.

Queen on the completion of the Scotch union they renewed in solemn language the request which they had made in 1703. "May God long preserve that life on which your people's happiness so much depends. May He put it in your royal heart to add greater strength and lustre to your crown by a yet more comprehensive union."[1]

In this year the Lords also congratulated the Queen on the Scotch union. After stating that that union would be an effectual means of quieting the empire, they proceed:—"May your Majesty go on and extend your favour to all your subjects till none are excluded from so great a blessing, but such as, by their own frowardness or disaffection to the public good, bar themselves from the general advantages of your Majesty's glorious reign; and we do hope your Majesty's unparalleled goodness and wisdom will conquer even those, and make them sensible of their true interest."[2]

These advances of the Irish Parliament were coldly received by the Queen and her ministers, who would not listen to the proposal of a union with Ireland. The reason of this short-sighted policy was that no danger was apprehended from a subordinate legislature. As long as the Irish Parliament was regarded as dependent on that of England, and English laws were considered to bind the Irish subject, there was no fear of any divergence in legislative aims or enactments. It was the existence of two equal and independent voices

[1] *Commons Journals*, July 9th, 1707.
[2] *House of Lords Journals*, ii. 161.

in the empire which was dreaded, and which the experience of Scotland had shown to be dangerous to the unity of the State. The English Parliament had just ordered Molyneux's book to be burned for denying its authority over Ireland, and had administered a rebuke to the Irish Assembly for venturing to claim legislative independence in re-enacting an English law which had been expressly made to bind Ireland.[1]

It is remarkable that the penal code was enacted by the Irish Parliament after their ineffectual attempts to obtain a legislative union with England. That body saw that the English connection was the only security of the Irish Protestants, and, as they were unable to draw it as close as they desired, they considered that the political power of the Catholics was incompatible with Protestant security, and that it was necessary to reduce them to a state of inability. Penal and disqualifying laws are hateful to us all, but our hatred of such restrictions should not prevent us from doing historical justice to the Protestant community and Parliament of Ireland, and from duly estimating the difficulties of their situation. In 1702, when the first Parliament of Anne met, fourteen years had not elapsed since the last determined attempt of the Catholics to root out of Ireland the name and the religion of Protestants; since the Catholics had thrown off the rule of England, and

---

[1] A bill for "the better security of her Majesty's person and government," re-enacting an English Act for abrogating the oath of supremacy in Ireland, had been lately transmitted from Ireland to England.

united themselves with her enemy, France; and since a persecution of the Protestants "as cruel as that of Languedoc"[1] had raged in every part of Ireland which owned the authority of the Catholic Government.[2] Penal laws against the Catholics stood on very different grounds in England and in Ireland. In England, the Protestants were as a hundred to one; in Ireland, they were as one to four, or even in a still greater disproportion. There was in England but little danger to be feared from a body which was so small and inconsiderable, but in Ireland the Catholics formed an overwhelming majority hostile to the Protestants and the English connection. What in England bore the appearance of persecution might in Ireland be considered a justifiable and necessary policy. There was not a member in either House of the Irish Parliament of 1702, which commenced the enactment of the Penal Code, of forty years of age and upwards, who had not suffered in person or estate from the violence and cruelty of the Catholics during their tenure of power from 1686 to 1690, or who had not witnessed scenes of oppression and outrage. The vast majority of the Lords and Commons who met in 1702 had had their estates forfeited, or they themselves had been, without a crime, without a trial, or possibility of

---

[1] Macaulay.
[2] In his "Instructions to the Commissioners of Oyer and Terminer," James II. himself bewails the general desolation of the land, and " the many robberies, oppressions, and outrages committed through all parts of the kingdom to the utter ruin thereof, and to the great scandal of the Government as well as of Christianity." - App. to King's *State of the Protestants.*

pardon,[1] condemned to the scaffold or the block.[2] Each individual among them had seen the Protestants disarmed, excluded from the army, and exposed to the outrages of an uncivilised and infuriated peasantry; the Courts of Justice handed over to their declared enemies; the whole executive power of the country transferred to the Catholics;[3] and every corporation in the kingdom practically closed to the Protestants. These are historical facts which cannot be gainsaid, and which it is our bounden duty to keep in mind when we judge the Parliament of Ireland and the Protestant community in that country. If the Parliament of England and the English people, with no immediate sense of danger, sanctioned penal laws against the Catholics of England, how much more natural was it that the Protestants of Ireland, scattered among a population hostile to them, their religion, and the English connection, should seek to

[1] By the great Act of Attainder James II., very much to his indignation, was precluded from pardoning any person mentioned in it.

[2] By this Act seventy-three members of the House of Lords, and the great majority of the Commons, were condemned to death. The number of persons attainted and doomed were, 2 archbishops; 1 duke; 63 temporal lords; 22 ladies; 7 bishops; 85 knights and baronets; 83 clergymen; and 2,182 esquires, &c. In fact, the whole Protestant peerage and gentry of Ireland were at one sweep condemned to death. The Act was concealed for some months, till the time limited for surrender had expired, so that, as the king could not pardon, there was no possibility of escape. Macaulay; Archbishop King. *List of the Persons Attainted in the Parliament of Ireland*, 1689. London, 1690.

[3] In 1687 there was but one Protestant sheriff in all Ireland, Charles Hamilton, and he was appointed in mistake for another of the same name who was a Catholic.

fortify themselves by disqualifying laws against those whom they believed to be their irreconcilable enemies.

The dangers and difficulties arising from the existence in Ireland of two nations differing in religion, customs, and traditions; and the possibility of independent Parliaments taking divergent paths, concurred with economical considerations in disposing the best and clearest heads in both countries to desire a legislative union or incorporation of the two kingdoms. From about the year 1670 we find a long list of distinguished writers and thinkers who recommend such a union. It would swell these pages unduly if all were mentioned; we shall therefore only quote the opinions of the principal ones.

In 1676 the Irish Council of Trade, in a report to the Lord Lieutenant, recommended an incorporate union on the plan of that between England and Wales.

In the same year Sir William Petty advised such a union. "May not," says he, "the three kingdoms be united into one and equally represented in Parliament? Might not the taxes be equally applotted and directly applied to their ultimate use? And why is not that natural and firm union made between the two [English and Irish] peoples?" And again, "If both kingdoms were under one legislature, power, and Parliament, the members whereof should be proportionable in power and wealth of each nation, there would be no danger such a Parliament should do anything to the prejudice of the English interest in Ireland, nor could the Irish ever complain of partiality when they shall be freely and proportionably represented in all Parliaments."

In 1694 Sir William Brewster thus speaks, "Though the sea part us, may not laws make us one, so that Ireland may be more profitable to England in general than Wales, or than any county is to the whole in its proportion? Keeping Ireland a separate kingdom hath supported the Irish in the pretence of their right to it. But if their Parliaments were abolished, and the kingdom united, we should become one people which we never can be while we live under different laws and governments."

In 1698 the celebrated Molyneux sighed for a legislative union. The whole of his little but famous book may be condensed into a single sentence. Ireland, argues Molyneux, is not bound by Acts of the English Parliament, because she is not represented there. Would to Heaven she were! A few lines of his own sum up the gist of his treatise. "If from these last-mentioned records it be concluded that the Parliament of England may bind Ireland, it must also be allowed that the people of Ireland ought to have their representatives in the Parliament of England. *And this, I believe, we should be willing enough to embrace; but this is an happiness we can hardly hope for.*"[1]

The first edition of this book was published by the author himself in 1698. It is significant that an edition was published in 1782 with the words which we have italicised omitted.[2]

In 1703, about the time when the Irish legislature

[1] *The Case of Ireland*, edition 1698, p. 17.
[2] The imposition was detected by Mr. Johnson in his *Reasons for Adopting a Union*, one of the Union pamphlets.

was unsuccessfully soliciting a union with England, Mr., afterwards Lord, Molesworth, a member of the Irish Commons and Chairman of one or more of the Committees that addressed the Queen on this subject, thus speaks :—" The ease and advantage which would be gained by uniting our own three kingdoms upon equal terms (for upon unequal it would be no union) is so visible, that if we had not the example of those masters of the world, the Romans, before our eyes, one would wonder that our own experience, in the instance of uniting Wales to England, should not convince us, that although both sides should incredibly gain by it, yet the rich and opulent country, to which such addition is made, would be the greater gainer."

In 1735 the great Irishman, Bishop Berkeley, published his queries. These queries leave no doubt as to the author's opinion on the subject of a union with England. We shall quote but one of them. " Whether anything can hurt us more than jealousy between England and Ireland, and whether it be not the interest of both nations to become one people, and whether either be sufficiently apprised of this ? "

In 1749, in his remarkable essay, *On the Causes of the Decline of Foreign Trade*, Sir Matthew Decker advocated a legislative union and a complete abolition of trade restrictions between England and Ireland. " By a union with Ireland no discontent could arise, but a general improvement spread over the three kingdoms without prejudice to each other."

In the year 1751 a very able plea for a union with Great Britain was published in Dublin. The publication was attributed to an Irish nobleman of large possessions. Its title was, *A Proposal for Uniting the Kingdoms of Great Britain and Ireland.* The author explains his idea of a union in these words :—" I do not mean a federal and partial union, but a complete incorporation of the two kingdoms inseparably and perpetually united; formed into one government under the same king and the same laws, and represented by the same Parliament; enjoying the same privileges and immunities, confined to the same restrictions, prohibitions, and regulations in trade; having the same alliances, the same enemies; and paying an equal proportion of taxes, customs, excise—both in peace and war—that in all instances they may become one people in affection as well as interest."

In 1767 Postlethwayt, an able commercial writer, strongly advocated a union of Ireland and Great Britain. "Bodies politic, like natural ones, are so far strong and potent, as all their limbs are firmly knit and well united, and equally fed and nourished; and while Ireland shall continue excluded from the favours, rights, and privileges, which her fellow subjects in England, Wales, and Scotland, so happily enjoy, she cannot prosper herself as she would otherwise do, and, therefore, cannot so much contribute as she might to the general wealth, strength, and security, of the whole State. If we dispassionately weigh these things, a union will appear in every view desirable by both kingdoms."

In 1775 Josiah Tucker, the well-known Dean of Gloucester, added his voice in favour of such a union.

"For example, the two great islands of Britain and Ireland, which are only separated by a narrow sea, ought not to be separated at all by different governments, laws, or Parliaments. No good reason upon earth can be given for such a separation. And it has long been the ardent wish of every true patriot in both nations to see them united."

We now come to the *clarum et venerabile nomen* of Adam Smith. "By a union with Great Britain Ireland would gain, besides the freedom of trade, other advantages much more important, and which would much more than compensate any increase of taxes that might accompany that union. By the union with England the middling and inferior ranks of people in Scotland gained a complete deliverance from the power of an aristocracy which had always before oppressed them. By an union with Great Britain the greater part of the people of all ranks in Ireland would gain a complete deliverance from a much more oppressive aristocracy. An aristocracy not founded, as that of Scotland, in the natural and respectable distinctions of birth and fortune, but in the most odious of all distinctions, those of religious and political prejudices—distinctions which, more than any other, animate both the insolence of the oppressors and the hatred and indignation of the oppressed, and which commonly render the inhabitants of the same country more hostile to one another than those of different countries ever are. Without an union with Great Britain the inhabitants of Ireland are not likely for many ages to consider themselves as one people."

In 1785, three years after the independence of Ireland had been declared, Dean Tucker again recurs to the consideration of this matter. "A real union and incorporation with Ireland is certainly a most desirable thing; but, according to the present situation of affairs, and men's tempers and dispositions, this is an event more to be wished for than to be expected. Nevertheless, when many of those obstacles, which now appear so formidable, shall be smoothed by the lenient hand of time, and when a mutual intercourse between England and Ireland shall confer mutual benefits on each other, it will then be found that the only thing remaining towards completing the commercial and political system, and towards giving strength and security, consistence and stability, to the whole, will be to unite under one legislature, to form one Parliament, and to become one people."

It is the province of the speculative inquirer to work out and suggest the reforms which the changing life of a nation requires. It is the province of the statesman to give effect to those reforms in legislation. And it becomes his immediate duty to do so, when his reason and conscience declare that they are necessary to the prosperity of the people whom he governs, and that the fulness of time has come for carrying them into operation. Was it possible for an English minister to shut his ears to the unanimous voice of so many distinguished thinkers on the subject of a union, for there was not a single opinion against it? But Pitt, in desiring a union, was not influenced merely by his own opinion, or by those of others. He had the experience of the Empire to guide him; and, in addition, the interposition of Great Britain was rendered absolutely necessary by the necessities of Ireland in 1799.

The existence of two independent Parliaments in the Empire had already been proved, by the case of Scotland, to be a source of extreme danger to the State. We shall hereafter consider the symptoms of separation shown by the Irish Parliament within a few years of the Declaration of Independence in 1782, but in this place we are speaking of Scotland. In the beginning of the reign of Anne a quarrel, arising principally from trade jealousy, broke out between England and Scotland. A Scotch company had been established for forming a settlement on the Spanish Main, avowedly to enable the northern kingdom to share the wealth and rival the trade of England. The settlement miscarried after having nearly caused a war between England and Spain, and this attempt and its failure produced great irritation and many controversies between the sister countries. The next step was the passing of the Act of Security by the Scotch Parliament. This Act declared that until provision was made for settling the rights and liberties of the Scotch nation, independently of English interests, the successor to the Scotch crown should not be the same person that was possessed of the crown of England. This Act was succeeded by an order for arming and training the subjects of Scotland. The Act of Security was looked upon in England as a declaration of war. The Parliament of England addressed the Queen to give orders for fortifying the towns on the northern frontier, for arming the militia of the northern counties, and for stationing regular forces in that part of the kingdom. At the same time an English Act was passed declaring the natives of Scotland aliens, unless that country should settle the crown on the House of Hanover by the 24th of December in the next year. Twenty-four men-of-war were fitted out, and orders were given them to seize Scotch ships trading with France under an Act which the Scots had lately passed allowing a trade with that country, then at war with England. Defoe tells us it was a case of "union or war; the animosities on both sides being raised to such a pitch that they could no longer have remained in the usual medium of peace."[1] Fortunately both kingdoms saw that two independent Parliaments were incompatible with their common safety, and the great measure of a Union was at last, after so many unsuccessful attempts, accomplished.

The intervention of Great Britain was imperatively called for by the state of Ireland. The rebellion of 1798 was essentially a different movement in the North and South. In the North, where the minds of men had been excited by the French Revolution, and a change in the system or form of government was desired, it was little more than a flash in the pan, which a few regiments would have extinguished.[2] But in the South, the

[1] *Hist. of the Union,* &c. 83.
[2] "The mere republicans submitted at once in the North. The papist fanatics are hardly to be subdued at all. They call the body

rebellion assumed the mixed complexion of a religious war and a *jacquerie*. There the peasantry, without leaders and without ammunition,[1] rushed into the bloody contest, during which all the worst passions of the two communities, the Protestants and the Catholics, were let loose. Their internecine quarrel was accompanied by the horrors which almost invariably attend outbursts of religious rancour. The outrages and atrocities of the Irish yeomanry and the Fencibles[2] were fully equalled by the barbarities of the peasantry. Both parties were infuriated against each other, and every sense of mercy or humanity was deadened or forgotten. The conflict was fast becoming a war of extermination,[3] when Great Britain intervened and

in the mountains the Irish and Catholic army."—Secretary Cooke to Wickham, *Corn. Corr.* ii. 363. "The actual movements of the conspiracy appeared almost exclusively in Ulster, where no religious motive was so much as pretended, and where the Roman Catholics, in particular, seemed disposed to distinguish themselves by keeping aloof from combination."—Alexander Knox, *Political Circumstances of Ireland*.

[1] Plowden, vol. ii. pt. ii. 687.

[2] The admirable conduct of the British regulars in this rebellion should never be forgotten. "The respect and veneration with which I heard the names of Hunter, Skeret, and Stewart . . . . pronounced, and the high encomiums passed on the Scotch and English regiments, under whose protection the misguided partisans of rebellion were enabled to return in safety to their homes, convinces me that the salvation of the country was as much owing to the forbearance, humanity, and prudence of the regular troops as to their discipline and bravery. The moment the militia, yeomanry, and Orangemen were separated from the army, confidence was restored."—Wakefield's *Ireland*, ii. 372.

[3] " The rebellion in 1798 would have been a war of extermination if it had not been for the strong and merciful interposition of Great

restored some degree of order. But the seeds of lasting hatred had been planted, for blood always leaves behind it the germs of future dissension, and, if the Union had not taken place, there would have been on Irish soil two nations bent on mutual destruction.

The three principal objects which Pitt had in view in pressing forward the Union were : to restore peace and put an end to the dissensions which distracted Ireland ; to admit the Catholics into the constitution by granting emancipation; and to consolidate the power and resources of the Empire by uniting all its subjects into one people, and by removing the causes of disaffection and alienation.[1]

Britain."—Lord Clare in the House of Lords, February 10th, 1800. "The choice of Father Roche (as a general of the rebels) shows how much the warfare had now altered its complexion and began to assume the form of a fanatic and religious crusade."—Plowden, vol. ii. pt. ii. 735. "In general we succeeded (in pleading with the rebels for the Protestants) for the first fortnight. After that the evil sanguinary spirit broke loose, and no protection availed . . . . in vain did we urge humanity, charity, religion, mercy."—Dr. Caulfield, Catholic Bishop of Ferns, quoted, Plowden, *ib.* p. 749. "In the South, where nearly the whole population is Roman Catholic, the contest assumed the appearance of a religious war rather than that of a rebellion."—Wakefield, ii. 365.

[1] See his speech on the Union, January 31st, 1799.

CHAPTER II.

State of the representation of Ireland between 1793 and 1800.—
Compared with that of England.—With that of Scotland.

To the English or Scotch inquirer Irish politics have always presented a difficult problem. The key to the problem is, that there are in Ireland, included under the generic term of Irish, two separate nations differing in origin, in religion, and in traditions: the Protestants and the Catholics. The Protestants are, for the most part, descendants of English or Scotch settlers; the Catholics are Celtic by blood or by traditions.

The Protestants have ever been attached to the British connection. For a short interval the Presbyterians of the North coquetted with republican sentiments and the United Irishmen. But the religious complexion which the rebellion assumed in the South, and particularly in Wexford, converted them to a man. They became almost universally Orangemen.[1] In June, 1799, Lord Castlereagh wrote to the Duke of Portland: "The province of Ulster comprises at this moment a numerous body of determined loyalists. The yeomanry equals in number, and far exceeds in effectiveness, that

[1] *Cast. Corr.* ii. 326.

of the other three provinces. They have of late been considerably augmented, and I am justified by the opinion of the officers commanding in that district in stating to your Grace that Ulster can be secured by its own yeomanry, and even furnish a considerable body of infantry well adapted to serve as light troops to act with the regular army against the common enemy."

At the time of the Union the population of Ireland was between four and five millions. Of these 800,000 were Protestants, the rest were Catholics. It must however be remembered that the estimates of the population before the institution of the census are nothing more than rough guesses. The Hearth money collectors gave it at 2,845,932 in the year 1785. Gervase Bushe computed it at 4,040,000 in 1788, an enormous increase of 1,200,000 in three years wholly unaccounted for. In 1791, the Hearth money collectors made it 4,206,612. Thomas Newenham estimated it at 5,359,456 in 1805. Grattan in 1782 stated it was 2,600,000; afterwards he raised his estimate to 4,000,000. Mr. Foster in 1799 was of opinion that it was four and a half millions, and in the same year Plunket thought it was between four and five millions.

The House of Lords was entirely Protestant, no Catholic sitting in it. The Irish peerage then consisted of about 210 members, more than forty of whom were in no way connected with Ireland.[1]

The House of Commons consisted of 300 members, and was also entirely Protestant. Sixty-four members were returned by the counties; 236 were returned by

[1] Portland to Lord Cornwallis.—*Corn. Corr.* iii. 214.

118 cities, towns, and boroughs, including the University of Dublin. Each constituency was represented by two members.

Though the Catholics of Ireland were not capable of sitting in Parliament, they yet enjoyed a very considerable amount of political power. The Irish electorate was out of all proportion to the population and resources of the kingdom when compared with either England or Scotland. Previous to 1793 the franchise was limited to Protestants, and the qualification for the county vote was the same as in England, a clear forty shillings freehold. Before that year the number of such voters was about 50,000, while in the cities, towns or boroughs the number of electors was about 20,000.[1] The act of 1793 admitted Catholic forty shilling freeholders, to the vote, and effected what was little short of a revolution in the electorate, at once tripling its number. This extraordinary change was brought about in the following manner. It had long been the habit in Ireland to let the land of the country on leases for lives.[2] The passion for acquiring political influence had induced landlords to create freehold tenures for the purpose of multiplying votes on their properties. As there was no expectation at that time of Catholics being admitted to the vote, this custom of granting freehold tenures was extended to them, after the penal laws had been

---

[1] See *State of the Representation* submitted to the Volunteer Convention, Dublin, 1784.

[2] "Almost all the lands of the country are let for lives, so that almost every peasant has a freehold tenure."—Sir L. Parsons, *Parl. Deb.* xiii. 213.

relaxed, and they were enabled to hold such estates.[1] The consequence was that nearly every peasant had a freehold tenure. Then came the Act of 1793, and at one blow a clear Catholic majority was established in the counties, and this at a time, when that body had not in their possession one-fiftieth part of the real, nor one-twentieth part of the personal property of the nation.[2]

A few instances of the changes made in the counties will show us the prodigious alteration effected by the Act. Before 1793 there were in Downshire 6,000 voters; shortly after there were 30,000. Tyrone county, before the Act, had 3,000 voters; shortly after it, 20,000. Cork county, before the Act, had 3,000 freeholders entitled to vote; after it, 20,000. The freeholders in County Galway were, before the Act, 700; shortly after it, 4,000. And Donegal had, before the Act, 3,000; and after it, 9,000.[3] In 1809, ten Irish counties, not including the wealthiest, Dublin, had upwards of 112,000 registered county voters.[4] At the time of the Union, the Irish county

---

[1] "Mr. Herbert says that a lease of lives was made to give the privileges of a freehold without any expectation of Catholics ever being admitted to vote. The law was established at a time when they were not permitted to take such leases, and for the purpose of giving the Protestants a decided majority over them. Afterwards the Catholics were allowed to possess freehold leases, and thus they obtained elective franchise."—Wakefield, ii. 611.

[2] *Parl. Deb.* xiii. 215.

[3] See and compare *State of Irish Representation* and Wakefield's *Ireland*, ii. 300-310.

[4] Wakefield's *Ireland*, ii. 300-310.

electorate must have numbered 200,000, if not more.[1]

In the larger constituencies of the cities and towns, which were more or less open, the influence of the Catholics had before 1800 become great. We can see this, by comparing the number of voters in these towns before 1793 with the number as given in the Parliamentary return in 1829.[2] It must be remembered that there was no change in the electoral laws between 1793 and 1829, and any increase in the population of the towns will not account for the much greater increase in the voters. Before 1793 the number of electors in Cork was 1,200; in 1829, 2,750. In Downpatrick, before 1793, the number was 250; in 1829, 2,180; In Newry before 1793, between 600 and 700; in 1829, 2,472. In Drogheda before 1793, 500; in 1829 1,143. In Dungarvan before 1793, 120; in 1829, 1708. In Galway before 1793, between 600 and 700; in 1829, 2,300. In Limerick, at the same times, 1,500 and 3,200.

The case of Newry will illustrate the change effected by the Act of 1793 in the Catholic influence in the

---

[1] In the debates on this Act, Sir Lawrence Parsons foretold this enormous increase. "In some counties where there are but 2,000 electors now, you will, if this bill passes, have 10,000; in others 20,000, in others 30,000, and I am well informed, in the county of Cork alone you will have 50,000; that is, half what I have stated the whole elective body to be of all the counties in England."— *Parl. Deb.* xiii. 213.

[2] See and compare the numbers as given in the *State of the Representation* laid before the Convention in 1784, and the Parliamentary returns, quoted in Lynch's *Law of Election*, p. 74.

open towns. Before the Act, this town had between six and seven hundred voters, all Protestants. In 1799 the Catholics were able to turn the election. In that year Mr. Corry, Chancellor of the Exchequer, stood for the town, and was opposed by Mr. Ball, a warm anti-Unionist. The Catholic Archbishop of Dublin requested Dr. Lennan, the Catholic Bishop of Dromore, to use his influence in favour of the Unionist candidate. We have the answer of the Bishop announcing the result. "Mr. Ball," he writes to the Archbishop, "with his partisans, after canvassing the town for eight days, declined the poll and surrendered yesterday. The Catholics stuck together like the Macedonian phalanx, and with ease were able to turn the scale in favour of the Chancellor of the Exchequer. He is very sensible of the efficacy of your interference and their steadiness."[1]

But in the smaller or private boroughs the Catholics had as yet no influence. Though the Act of 1793 had opened corporations to them, sufficient time had not elapsed to enable them to make their way into these citadels of Protestantism. Whatever we may think of the Protestant constitution and establishment then existing in Ireland, we must acknowledge that the private or rotten boroughs were their only protection.

The political position of the Irish Catholics, between 1793 and the Union, then, was this. They could command the greater number of the county elections throughout the island; they were rapidly becoming the majority in the open cities and towns, but they were excluded, not by law, but by custom, from the private

[1] *Cast. Corr.* ii. 168.

boroughs. If the attention of this body had not been distracted from purely political aims by the conspiracy of the United Irishmen and the disturbances of 1798, and if the private or rotten boroughs had not remained Protestant, the Catholics would have had control of all Irish matters by the year 1800.

Both the social and political situation of the Irish Catholics have been misrepresented, and the restrictions under which they laboured have been greatly exaggerated. It may be useful to compare the position of a Catholic in Ireland after 1793 with that of his co-religionist in England or Scotland. In those countries Catholics were excluded from office and the franchise. In Ireland they were admissible to all civil and military places of trust under the Crown, with the exception of about thirty of the highest executive offices of the State.[1] The Test and Corporation Acts had also been repealed in their favour in Ireland, while in England and Scotland these instruments of exclusion were retained for many years subsequently to 1800. In England, a Catholic was, as in Ireland, excluded from Parliament, but in the former country he could not take a degree at one of the universities, or become a member of a corporation, nor could he rise in the Army or Navy above the rank of Lieutenant. In Ireland every law pressing on the Catholic had been relaxed,[2] and he

---

[1] 33 Geo. III. Irish c. 21, §§ 7, 9.
[2] The provision in respect to the possession of arms by the Catholics can hardly be termed an exception, for every Catholic entitled to a freehold of 10*l.* per annum, or to personal property of the value of 300*l.*, could obtain a license on payment of 6*d.*

was invested with all the privileges possessed by Protestants, except that he could not sit in Parliament, or enjoy a few great offices without taking the same oaths of qualification as were taken by Protestants. In no country in the world where there was an established religion did the nonconforming subject enjoy a situation comparable to that of the Irish Catholic. Even the condition of the Protestant Dissenters in England was inferior to his. There, a Presbyterian, member of a church established in another part of the island, to qualify himself for the humblest office, was obliged to communicate in the form of a religion to which he did not belong. And the other Dissenters, such as Quakers and Unitarians, were in a situation far inferior to that of the Irish Catholic. The franchise, too, was only enjoyed by Protestant Dissenters in England in a qualified manner, for they were debarred from exercising it in thirty corporations and towns which returned members to Parliament.[1]

Of the 118 Irish cities, towns, and boroughs which existed before the Union, some were more or less open, that is free from external influence or patronage. The following had large constituencies: Dublin, between 4,000 and 5,000 electors; Cork, about 2,000; Waterford, 1,000; Limerick, about 2,000; Londonderry, between 600 and 700; Carrickfergus, 900; Drogheda, about 500; Newry about 1,500;

Catholics, too, were openly enrolled among the Volunteers, and were possessed of arms without license."—*Parl. Deb.* xiii. 107.

[1] Petition of the Friends of the People, 1793.

Youghal, 200; Antrim, 250; Downpatrick, about 1,000; and Fethard in Tipperary 900.[1]

The first eight of these, Dublin, Cork, Waterford, Limerick, Londonderry, Carrickfergus, Drogheda, and Newry were quite open, as was also the University of Dublin.[2]

Of the towns which were partially open, Antrim was comparatively free though influenced by Lord Massareene; Lisburn was in the same position to Lord Hertford. Of Mallow the principal patrons were the Jephson family. Youghal, as most of its freeholders resided at a distance of sixty miles, was entirely in the hands of Lord Shannon. Wexford by "manœuvring of the Corporation" had come under the influence of a single individual. In Downpatrick and Kinsale Lord de Clifford was able to return the four members. Dundalk had been for some years struggling for freedom with the Clanbrassil family. It appears that the struggle went against the town, for though it was described in 1784 as having 700 electors, we find in the parliamentary return

[1] The following are the numbers of electors in these towns in 1784 and 1829:—

	1784	1829		1784	1829
Dublin	4,000	5,000	Drogheda	500	1,143
Cork	1,200	2,750	Newry, between 600 & 700		2,472
Waterford	1,000	1,286	Galway	600	2,300
Limerick	"many hundreds"	3,200	Mallow	.	550
Londonderry	700	650	Downpatrick	250	2,180
Carrickfergus	900	860	Youghal	200	242

[2] Of this constituency the Report on the representation says, "electors 70 scholars and 22 fellows, in all 92, who cannot be corrupted even by the present Provost." The Provost was Hely Hutchinson, against whom Duigenan wrote his *Pranceriana* and *Lacrymæ Academicæ*.

of 1829 that there were in the town only thirty-two electors; Athlone and Fethard acknowledged patrons.

In the rest of the boroughs the right of election was generally limited to the Corporation, a body usually of thirteen persons. Even in the towns which, from their importance, though not open, were retained to send members to the Imperial Parliament, this was the case, and their condition was not changed till the Municipal Reform Act in 1840. Thus in Belfast, Armagh, Bandon, Carlow, Sligo, Ennis, and Tralee respectively the number of electors was thirteen, in Dungannon twelve, and in Enniskillen and Portarlington fifteen.

Four boroughs were in an exceptional position. Three of them had become close though owned by no one, and the fourth was a thoroughly venal one. St. Canice, or Irishtown, a part of Kilkenny city, had succumbed to the influence of the Bishop of Ossory, as had Old Leighlin to that of the Bishop of Ferns. Clogher had long been under the patronage of the Bishop, but it regained its independence on the very eve of the Union, when the two nominees of the Bishop were unseated.[1] Swords, with its 160 electors, was free from external influence, but sold itself on every opportunity.

With the exception of these four boroughs, and also with the exception of the cities and towns wholly or partially open, the Irish boroughs had been originally, or had become, private property. Their history is as follows :—

The great majority of Irish boroughs had always been mere villages. In the last Parliament of Elizabeth,

[1] *Journals House of Commons*, March 29th, 1800.

when writs were issued to thirty-six places only, many of these places which sent representatives were insignificant. They were chosen because they were walled towns, or occupied positions favourable for defence or commerce. In the reign of this Queen seventeen counties were added to the existing ones, and in the following reign all Ireland became shire ground. James I. created forty-six new boroughs;[2] and Charles I., Charles II., James II., and Anne afterwards increased the number by thirty-six. So that more than two-thirds of the boroughs were created by the Stuarts. James I. not only created new boroughs, but recalled the charters of some of the old towns and granted new ones. In all his fifty-three charters he prescribed the number of citizens who were to have a vote, and limited that number within the narrowest bounds. He separated the small class incorporated by the grant as much as possible from the inhabitants at large, and generally named the individuals who were to be the first mayor, sheriffs, and burgesses. Hence arose a system most favourable to direct nomination, self-election, and thorough exclusiveness.[3] Grattan tells us that most of the boroughs erected by James I. were

[1] In the reign of Henry VIII. the English Pale comprised four counties only.

[2] When the King was remonstrated with for making so many he replied: "What is it to you whether I make many or few boroughs? My Council may consider the fitness if I require it. But what if I had created 40 noblemen and 400 boroughs? The more the merrier, the fewer the better cheer."—*Cur. Hiber.* i. 308.

[3] Gale, *Ancient Corporation System.* Lynch, *Law of Election in Ancient Cities, &c., of Ireland.*

intended to be private property, that this appears from the grants themselves, and that those created by Charles II. were granted with a view to personal favour.[1]

With respect to those boroughs which were not originally granted to individuals as private property, it is easy to understand how they became the possessions of patrons. The number of electors was so small that the nomination of a member came to be considered as an exclusive and valuable right which it was desirable to limit to as few as possible. Accordingly the appointment of new burgesses was purposely neglected, and their succession was allowed to lapse. By death, removal of families from the town, or decay of the place, the number of electors was still further reduced. In 1784 there were only three resident electors in the five boroughs of the county of Donegal, one, a publican in Lifford, one in the town of Donegal, and one in Ballyshannon, none in Killybegs or St. Johnstown. There were no resident electors in Newtownlimavady, Castlebar, Clonmines, Old Leighlin, Portarlington, Carrick, Tulsk, Longford, or Fethard.[2] In Newtownards, Jamestown, Enniscorthy, Coleraine, Monaghan, and Mullingar only one in each. In Duleek there was not one resident in the town or even in the county. The majority of the electors of Kinsale resided in another province, Ulster. Of the 150 freemen of Dingle only two resided in the town and not more than ten in the county. In many other boroughs only two, three, or

[1] Speech on reform.—*Parl. Deb.* xiii. 160.
[2] There were two Fethards, one in Wexford and one in Tipperary.

five electors were resident. Harristown and Bannow were totally uninhabited. Jamestown, from a town, had become "a wretched depopulated village," and Carysfort had "gone entirely to ruin and decay, its electors all non-resident."[1] Under such circumstances these boroughs naturally gravitated into the power of the lord of the soil or the neighbouring proprietor, and were universally recognised as his private property, to be disposed of as he thought fit. To the credit of these acquirers it must be said that they rarely or never allowed a member who differed from them in political opinions to sit in one of their seats. At the time of the Union, the Ponsonbys exercised influence, direct or indirect, over twenty-two seats; Lord Downshire, and the Beresfords, respectively, over nearly as many. Lord Longueville claimed Cork, Mallow, and six other seats; Lords Ely and Shannon had six; Lords Granard, Belmore, Clifden, and Abercorn four each. The Duke of Devonshire, Mr. Tighe, and Mr. Bruen had also each four.[2]

After their acquisition boroughs were looked upon as strictly private property, and treated as such. For many years before 1800 they had been bought and sold, bequeathed by will, or disposed of in family and marriage settlements. Their value was very great, though not comparable to that of the English pocket-boroughs.[3] They were considered to be advancements

---

[1] *Report on the Representation*, submitted to the Volunteer Convention, Dublin, 1784.

[2] *Corn. Corr.*, iii. 324.

[3] Gatton, in Surrey, was sold in 1774 for £75,000. May, *Const. Hist.*, i. 305.

for younger sons, and were readily saleable, particularly to aspiring barristers. About the year 1780 Belturbet was sold for £11,000. But their value was raised enormously by the Octennial Act. The chances of profit to a borough proprietor, over the sum given for a seat, were the dissolution of Parliament, and the death or removal by promotion of the sitting member. It is evident that an Act which limited the duration of Parliament, and thereby increased the number of vacancies, must have raised the pecuniary value of the boroughs. The distinction between the value of a borough and that of a seat must be kept in mind; between the perpetual right of nomination and a single sitting. The purchase of a borough, or half a borough, was an investment, the sale of a seat its produce. The value of a seat, though it also had risen with the value of the borough,[1] depended largely on the crisis, or the debate of a great question which interested the public. Grattan gave £2,000 for a seat in 1784 for a friend of his patron, Lord Charlemont.[2] In 1800 he again gave £2,400 for his seat at Wicklow.[3] In the same year Mr. Gould paid £4,000 for his seat at Kilbeggan,[4] and Lord Cornwallis states that at this time the Opposition offered £5,000 ready money for a vote.[5]

We must not hastily suppose that our forefathers were shocked at this system of representation. On the

---

[1] "I have heard that seats in this House, forty years ago, were obtained for 600*l*. I have heard they now cost 3,000*l*."—Grattan, 1793; *Parl. Deb.*, xiii. 162.
[2] *Grattan's Life*, iii. 191. [3] *Corn. Corr.*, iii. 161.
[4] *Ib.* iii. 182. [5] *Ib.* iii. 184.

contrary the great majority of them thought it an excellent one, and we shall shortly see that a similar system prevailed in England and Scotland. Parliamentary reform was never popular in Ireland. Flood's attempt brought about the fall of the Volunteers, who were the only large body that promoted it. His motion in 1783 to bring in a Reform Bill was unsupported by petitions from the people,[1] and was rejected by 150 votes to 77. When Grattan renewed the attempt in 1793, the majorities against it were overwhelming, 153 to 71, and 137 to 48, the first against the introduction of Grattan's resolution, the second against a subsequent motion of Mr. Forbes.[2] Again in 1794, a Bill for reform was unsupported[3] by petitions, and was thrown out by 142 votes to 44. And finally, when Mr. W. B. Ponsonby brought forward Grattan's plan for reform in 1797 he could only muster 30 votes against 170.[4]

In truth, it is difficult to see how any one at that time could think that reform of the parliamentary system was feasible in Ireland. Even if the political situation of the two parties in the kingdom had allowed it, there was no wealthy middle-class in the country who felt that they did not enjoy the influence in legislation which their position and intelligence fairly entitled them to claim. There were no captains of national industries, no great manufacturers, no commercial magnates, as in England, who were indignant at their exclusion from political power, and were ready to

[1] *Grattan's Life*, iii. 149. [2] *Parl. Deb.* xiii. 188, 245.
[3] *Parl. Deb.* xiv. 104. [4] *Ib.*, xvii. 570.

challenge the monopoly of legislation possessed by the landholders. Nor was there any strong, moral indignation at the parliamentary system, hardly a mere sentimental disapproval of its abuses. We find it difficult to repress a smile when we read that Grattan, who sat for a pocket-borough by the favour of a patron, and who bought a seat in 1784, and again in 1800, was the strenuous asserter of parliamentary reform. And that George Ponsonby, who, with his brother William, represented in the House of Commons a family which influenced twenty-two seats, and was himself the proprietor of a rotten borough, for which he received £15,000 compensation at the Union, was anxious to purify the legislature. The public would not believe that men who trafficked in boroughs to suit their own convenience were sincere, or that those who derived a large part of their importance from anomalies and abuses of the Parliamentary system were actuated by conscientious motives when they demanded its reform.

But there was one circumstance which, above all others, prevented parliamentary reform in Ireland, and that was the alarm of the Protestant legislature, and of the Protestant community. They saw with disquietude the rapid advances which the Catholics had made within a few years. They were aware that the political power of the country was being transferred to that body—that the county elections were at the disposal of that community—that its members were becoming possessed of power in the larger towns and constituencies; and that the private pocket-boroughs were the only remaining defences of their constitution and religious establishment.[1] Grattan, of whose gifts political foresight was not one, had made up his mind that the Catholics were not to be feared. The state of religious thought on the Continent, and the straits to which the victories of the French Republicans had reduced the Papal Court and Sovereign, led him to believe that the Catholic religion had lost its social and political influence.[2] He foresaw no danger in the admission of Catholics to Parliament, or in their overwhelming numbers. But this feeling was by no means shared by the Protestant community at large. That body feared that a Catholic Parliament would attack the existing constitution of Church and State, if not the Act of Settlement, which was the root of every title in Ireland, and that it might endanger their only safety, the connection with Great Britain. The result of these fears was, that they were resolved to maintain the existing order of things as long as it was possible to do so, and determined to resist all parliamentary reform which would destroy the safeguards of their constitution and establishment.

[1] "We may live to see boroughs, now disgraced with the epithet *rotten*, the only defence of the Protestants of Ireland."—Right Hon. Geo. Ogle, *Parl. Deb.* xiii. 248.

[2] "The indulgence we wish to give to Catholics can never be injurious to the Protestant religion. That religion is the religion of the State, and will become the religion of Catholics if severity does not prevent them." "What Luther did for us, philosophy has done in some degree for the Roman Catholics, and that religion has undergone a silent reformation."—Both quoted by Lecky, iv. 557.

With all its imperfections the Irish parliamentary system represented fairly the principal interests of the country, the land, the church, law, and commerce. Perhaps the land, and certainly the church, was over represented, though it must be remembered that there was little trade or commerce in Ireland. Lawyers were always numerous and influential in the Irish Parliament, and there were at least six Dublin bankers in the last legislature. The popular voice had a real, if not a controlling influence within its walls.[1] The Irish Houses were never able to resist the persistent wishes of the electoral body,[2] as was conclusively shown in the earlier stages of the Octennial Bill, and on several other occasions. Besides, the Irish were well aware that their own system was in some respects better than that of England, and that it was absolute perfection when compared with that of Scotland. It was better than the English system in two respects. The first was, that in Ireland the Catholics were admitted to the franchise, whereas they were excluded in England. The second was, a much larger proportion of the people participated in the privilege in Ireland. The population of England was, about the time of the Union, upwards of ten millions, that of Ireland, at the most, five millions. There was no comparison between the wealth and resources of the two kingdoms. Yet, the electorate was nearly as numerous in Ireland as in England, and if we preserve the proportion of the populations, we shall find that Ireland had about

---

[1] Lecky, iv. 370.   [2] Ib.

twice the number of electors which England had in 1800 and for thirty years after that date.

We cannot properly judge of the system of Irish representation which prevailed from 1793 to 1800 without comparing it with the contemporaneous arrangements which existed in England and Scotland. We shall therefore shortly consider the systems of representation in those countries.

"A stranger," said Lord John Russell in 1831, in his speech introducing the Reform Bill, "would be very much astonished if he were taken to a ruined mound and told that that mound sent two representatives to Parliament—if he were taken to a stone wall and told that three niches in it sent two representatives to Parliament—if he were taken to a park where no houses were to be seen, and told that that park sent two representatives to Parliament. But if he were told all this and were astonished at hearing it, he would be still more astonished if he were to see large and opulent towns, full of enterprise, and industry, and intelligence, containing vast magazines of every species of manufacture, and were then told that these towns sent no representatives to Parliament. Such a person would be still more astonished if he were taken to Liverpool, where there is a large constituency, and told 'here you will have a fair specimen of a popular election.' He would see bribery employed to the greatest extent, and in the most unblushing manner; he would see every voter receiving a number of guineas in a box as the price of his corruption."

In England a much smaller proportion of the population was represented than in Ireland. The majority in the House of Commons was, in 1793, said to be elected by less than fifteen thousand voters.[1] This statement was not exaggerated, for the Duke of Richmond declared in 1780 that not more than six thousand individuals returned a clear majority of the Commons.[2] About the time of the Union there were in Ireland two hundred thousand electors in the counties, beside those in the cities, towns, and boroughs, and more than a thirtieth part of the people was represented in Parliament.

No Catholic could vote in England, and by the operation of the Test laws even Protestant Dissenters were deprived of the franchise in thirty boroughs. Catholics and Dissenters enjoyed the privilege of the vote in Ireland.

Seventy English members were returned from thirty-five places where the elections were mere matters of form. Ninety were returned from forty-six places, in none of which the electors numbered more than fifty. Thirty-seven from places where the voters did not exceed a hundred, and fifty-two members were returned from places where the electors did not exceed two hundred.[3]

Cornwall and Wiltshire sent more borough members than Yorkshire, Lancashire, Warwickshire, Middlesex,

[1] Petition of the Friends of the People, presented by Mr., afterwards Lord Grey in 1793. This Society embraced men eminent in politics and literature, and twenty-eight members of Parliament, among whom were Mr. Grey and Mr. Erskine. May, *Const. Hist.* i. 334.   [2] *Ib.* i. 299.
[3] Petition of the Friends of the People.

Worcestershire and Somersetshire united. The borough members of Cornwall alone outnumbered those of Yorkshire, Rutland and Middlesex. This one county returned forty-four members, while the whole of Scotland had but forty-five representatives.[1]

If we turn to the question of patronage we shall find matters in a similar state to that which prevailed in Ireland. Eighty-four individuals, by their own immediate authority, returned one hundred and fifty-seven members. In addition to these a hundred and fifty members were returned at the recommendation of seventy influential persons. So that a hundred and fifty-four patrons returned a decided majority of the English members.[2] This was in 1793, in 1816 Oldfield tells us that three hundred and fifty-five members were returned by peers and influential commoners in England and Wales.[3]

The interference of peers in elections was as general in England as in Ireland. A hundred and fifty members owed their election entirely to this interference. Forty peers had acquired burgage tenures in many of the small boroughs, and were enabled by their own authority to return eighty-one members. The Duke of Norfolk was represented by eleven members, Lord Lonsdale by nine, Lord Darlington by seven, the Duke of Rutland, the

---

[1] Petition of the Friends of the People.
[2] The number of representatives from England and Wales was then 513, from Scotland 45. Cornwall sent 44 members. Oldfield, vi. 133. Petition of the Friends, &c.
[3] Total number of members returned by 87 peers in England and Wales, 218; by 90 commoners, 137. *Representative Hist.*, vi. 293.

Marquis of Buckingham, and Lord Carrington by six each.[1]

If we add to all this that there were ten places in England the members of which, sixteen in number, were returned by the patronage of Government, we shall have an idea of the system of representation which prevailed in England at the time of the Irish Union, and for thirty years later.[2]

The representation of Scotland was defective and anomalous in the highest degree. In the counties the great mass of the landholders and householders was excluded from all participation in the choice of members. The vote was severed from the land, and attached to a fictitious creation of the law known by the name of the "Superiority." So that the representatives of the landed interest might be elected by those who had no real or beneficial interest in the soil, and who were called "out-voters."[3] These "Superiorities" were openly bought and sold in the market, and were enjoyed independently of property or even of residence.[4]

Even so late as 1831 the total number of county electors in Scotland did not exceed two thousand five hundred.[5] The county of Argyll, with a population of a hundred thousand, had but a hundred and fifteen electors, of whom eighty-four had no land in the county. Caithness, with thirty thousand inhabitants, contained

[1] May, *Const. Hist.*, i. 277.
[2] These places were: Dartmouth 2, Dover 1, Harwich 2, Hythe 2, Windsor 1, Hampshire 2, Yarmouth 1, Queensborough 2, Rochester 1, Sandwich 2. Oldfield, vi. 292.
[3] Petition of the Friends, &c. [4] May, *Const. Hist.*, i. 295.
[5] *Ib.* i. 295.

forty-seven voters, of whom thirty-six had no real property in it. In Invernessshire, with a population of ninety thousand, there were but eighty-eight voters, of whom fifty were unconnected with the land. And the county of Bute, which contained a population of fourteen thousand, had twenty-one electors, of whom only one resided within it.[1]

With respect to the boroughs, everything that bore even the semblance of popular choice had long been done away with. The election of members was vested in magistrates and town councils that had constituted themselves into self-elected bodies, and had deprived the people of all participation in the privilege. Edinburgh and Glasgow had each a constituency of thirty-three persons. The constituencies of the sixty-six boroughs amounted to one thousand four hundred and forty. So that the entire electoral body of Scotland was not more than four thousand,[2] not a fiftieth part of the Irish electorate at or shortly after the Union.

In 1816 there was not a free seat in all Scotland. Of the forty-five members returned by that country thirty-one were returned by peers or peeresses, and fourteen by commoners.[3] No Catholic could vote at elections.

Humour often decides a question on which reason labours in vain. The story told by the Lord Advocate in 1831 to the House of Commons will illustrate the Scotch representation and its working. The county of Bute, as has been mentioned, had twenty-one electors, of whom one resided in the county. "At an election at

[1] May, *Const. Hist.* i. 295.   [2] *Ib.*
[3] Oldfield, *Rep. Hist.*, vi, 295.

Bute only one person attended the meeting except the sheriff and returning officer. He of course took the chair, constituted the meeting, called over the roll of freeholders, answered to his own name, took the vote as to the Preses, and elected himself. He then moved and seconded his own nomination, put the question as to the vote, and was unanimously returned."[1]

[1] *Hansard*, 3 *Ser.*, vii. 529, quoted by May, *Const. Hist.*, i. 297.

CHAPTER III.

Nature of the connection which existed between Great Britain and Ireland after 1782.—Its dangers.—Tendencies to separation, as shown in the refusal of a Commercial Treaty.—In the Regency question.—In actual and proposed Irish Legislation.

THE settlement of 1782 put an end to the degrading position in which Ireland stood with respect to Great Britain, and elevated her to the rank of an independent kingdom. By it the four grievances of which Ireland complained were removed. These grievances were—The claim of Great Britain to bind Ireland by her laws: The Appellate jurisdiction: the provisions of Poynings' law: and the perpetuity of the Mutiny Act. But these four grievances may be reduced to one, viz., the claim to bind Ireland by enactments made in the British Parliament, for the others were merely appurtenant to it. The Appellate jurisdiction fell with the legislative claim, and the other two were matters of internal arrangement. The settlement was final as to the only matters in dispute between the two countries, and it established fully and perfectly the constitution and legislative Independence of Ireland. It was not, however, preclusive of further measures which the legislatures of both countries might deem necessary for securing the permanence of the connection between them. It was not an abolition of the inherent powers of the two Parliaments, nor did it extinguish or abridge their deliberative or operative capacities. It is evident that it did not preclude independent Ireland or independent Great Britain from offering to, or accepting from, the other an International treaty; whether that treaty referred to commercial regulations or to such an Imperial arrangement as a Legislative Union.[1]

No attempt was ever made by Great Britain, as has been asserted, to violate the legislative independence of Ireland as established in 1782. On the contrary, it was scrupulously and loyally respected. Ireland was satisfied with the repeal of the Declaratory Act of George I.; Great Britain passed a law renouncing all legislative claims on Ireland. On every solemn occasion Great Britain seized the opportunity of declaring Ireland's legislative independence. In 1785, at the time of the proposed Commercial Treaty, the Bill, which was introduced into the English Parliament to carry out its provisions, pronounced that the Parliament of Ireland was alone competent to make laws binding on that kingdom. At the same time, both Houses of the British Parliament concurred in an address to the Crown containing an explicit declaration to the same effect. The stipulation required by Great Britain that Ireland should adopt England's commercial regulations and

---

[1] The babble about the "finality" of the settlement of 1782 is melancholy reading. Three questions only did or could arise respecting the Union—1. Were the two legislatures competent to enact it? 2. Was it of so great advantage to both nations as to make it desirable? 3. Was the time opportune?

re-enact them in her own legislature, was the strongest acknowledgment of Ireland's independence. In 1799, Pitt, in the British Parliament, declared that the Irish Parliament possessed the sole and uncontrolled right and discretion to reject or accept any proposal of a measure of Union, and stated that the British legislature was incompetent in any way to bind Ireland by its laws. Indeed, the recommendation of the Sovereign directed to the Irish Parliament in 1799 to take the project of Union into their consideration was a practical admission that they, and they alone, were competent to decide on such a question.

To have passed a statute in Great Britain, and acting under it, to have enforced a Union on Ireland, would have been a violation of Irish independence. Even a request from the former kingdom to Ireland that the latter should resume the dependent position she occupied before 1782, would not have been a violation of her independence, provided that request was accompanied by an acknowledgment of Ireland's absolute right to refuse or to grant the request. But nothing of this kind was done. The proposal of a Legislative Union was an offer made by one independent nation to another equally independent, and accepted by that other. Twice before, in 1703 and 1707, the Irish Parliament had proposed such a Union to Great Britain. If this proposal had been accepted by Great Britain, no one would presume to say that this acceptance would have affected her legislative independence, or even lowered her national prestige. How then can it be urged that the acceptance by Ireland of a similar offer destroyed her legislative independence? To assert that the Union of 1800 extinguished the legislative powers of Ireland, or lowered her Imperial dignity, is to confound independence with distinctness, and union with subordination. The voluntary union of two partners does not extinguish the individuality of either, or affect his personal worth. The addition of two numbers does not destroy or lessen the value of either of the constituent factors.

If rightly considered, it will be seen that the Legislative Union, though it put an end to Ireland's distinctness, secured for ever her legislative independence. Independent Ireland, by the Act of Union, and by the voice of her King, Lords and Commons, declared that from henceforth she would commix and unite her Parliament with that of Great Britain, and that the new Parliament, formed from this mixture, should for the future give laws to Irishmen. It is from this operative Act of Ireland's King, Lords, and Commons, that the power of the mingled or Imperial Parliament to bind the inhabitants of Ireland by its laws is derived. It is this, and this alone, which confers the authority upon the Imperial Parliament of making laws for Ireland, and in every Act of that Legislature the voice of Ireland is still heard, and her legislative independence is not dead, but daily makes itself known. For it is from the power which she conferred on the new Imperial Parliament that that Parliament has the right to legislate for the inhabitants of Ireland. Her mandate constitutes the Imperial Parliament, as far as Irish legislative matters are concerned, the agent or factor of Ireland, and makes that mixed legislature the native

Parliament of Ireland, as much as it is the native Parliament of Yorkshire or Scotland: as much her native Parliament as was that which sat in College Green.

The acknowledgment of Irish independence by Great Britain, and the settlement of 1782, were of the last importance to Ireland. For her independence enabled her to treat as an equal in the subsequent settlement of 1800, and to demand and exact as an equal fair and advantageous terms for a legislative union. It put her in a position to dictate the only alliance which she would accept. It was a necessary step, but only a step, in a movement, which, though it was to a certain extent controlled by individuals, did not originate with them. It arose from those tendencies which, though hidden from the immediate actors, give rise to and direct the development of societies. It sprang from the necessities of the two countries, and especially from the condition and circumstances of Ireland.

For an incorporate union, in some shape or other, was inevitable, and only a matter of the shortest time. Even if the connection between the two kingdoms, instead of being as faulty as the wit of man could devise, had been perfect—if every asperity between them had been smoothed, and the commercial intercourse had been freed from every cause of friction—if their tariff had been settled, duties equalised, the navigation laws relaxed, and all jealousies removed, an incorporation of the two countries would still have been necessary. Such a union was imperatively called for by the requirements of the Empire, and by those of Ireland herself. The repeated French invasions of Ireland, and the hostility of the Catholic community,[1] had taught Great Britain the necessity of guarding the door of the Empire, and of anticipating, by an incorporation of the country, the efforts of foreign enemies and the designs of domestic traitors. For Ireland the measure was absolutely essential. The Catholic question had already assumed gigantic proportions. The American War, the French Revolution, and the grant of the franchise to the Catholics in 1793, had advanced the question in almost a moment by fifty years. Like the gourd of the prophet, it had started up and ripened in a single night. It was a question which never could have been settled without a contest in a separate Ireland. The Protestant Parliament would not, indeed they could not, have granted complete emancipation, for the grant would have immediately led to a Catholic majority in the legislature. The Parliament was well aware of the danger of its position, and that Ireland could not exist an hour as a Protestant state without the support of England, or the continuance of disqualifying laws.[2] When England refused, or made no answer to the Irish request for a legislative union in 1703, the Irish Parliament, despair-

---

[1] "In Ireland the name of England and her power is universally odious. The Catholics are enemies to the English power from a hatred to the English name." Wolfe Tone to the French Directory. This gentleman had opportunities of knowing the truth, for he was for some years the Secretary of the Catholic Committee in Dublin, and was voted a sum of 1,500*l.* for his services by it.

[2] In 1785 a member thus explained their position to the House of Commons: "The assertion of my right honourable friend [Fitzgibbon, afterwards Lord Clare] is that this nation could not exist one hour as an independent Protestant state without the

ing of their power of maintaining themselves among a hostile people, resolved to reduce their opponents to political impotency by the enactment of the penal laws. It is a mistake to suppose that these laws were the result of a persecuting spirit or religious animosity. They sprang from political fears and disquietude. Fourteen years only had then elapsed since the Catholics had made a determined effort in 1689, the second within a period of fifty years, to root out the Protestant community from Ireland. In this effort they had deprived the Protestants of twelve million acres of their land, and by the infamous Act of Proscription, which no Catholic writer has ever reprobated, had doomed two thousand five hundred of their nobility, gentry and traders to "such pains of death, penalties, and forfeitures respectively as in cases of high treason are accustomed."[1] About the time of the Union it was the deliberate opinion of the vast majority of the Irish Parliament that laws disqualifying the Catholics from political power were necessary for their own safety.[2] This belief was not limited to the Irish Parliament, it was shared by many Liberal statesmen in England. In 1799 Canning

support of Great Britain. The House knows very well that they do not represent more than one-fourth of the people of Ireland, and that to that fourth the connection with England is essential. And I desire, gentlemen, to reflect that if the connection was broken the same representatives would not be found in Parliament. The salvation of this kingdom as a Protestant state depends on it." *Par. Reg.* v. 472.   [1] The words of the Act.

[2] The proposal to admit Catholics to Parliament in 1797 was rejected by a majority of 170 to 30.

intimated his opinion in the British Commons that if the Union with Ireland did not take place, it might be necessary to re-fortify the Protestant ascendency by reviving the old penal code against the Catholics. As long as this opinion prevailed, full emancipation was impossible, and the right of sitting in Parliament would not have been granted without a long struggle. It was a case of union with peace, or continued disqualification and civil contests. The Act of 1793, which conceded the franchise to Catholics, had brought the two communities face to face; the Catholics relying on their enormous numerical preponderance, the possession of more than two-thirds of the voting power of the country, and their hopes of foreign aid; the Protestants emboldened by their political ascendency and the knowledge that Great Britain would not desert them.[1] The two parties were infuriated against each other; maddened by their mutual wrongs and sufferings during the rebellion they were eagerly straining on the leash. Even the full emancipation of the Catholics would only have precipitated the contest and brought it to a head. For the question whether Ireland should be Protestant or Catholic would then have arisen, and would have been fought to the bitter end. There was but one way of keeping the peace between the discordant factions, and that was by an incorporate union. After such a union the demands of the Catholics might be safely conceded,

[1] "Two infuriated parties, contending for superiority, stood opposed to each other, and the Government of the country had a most favourable opportunity of becoming the mediator." Wakefield's *Ireland*, ii. 360.

but in a separate Ireland there was nothing to look forward to but national dissension, and perhaps a bloody convulsion followed by a re-conquest. Happily, as will be seen hereafter, no sooner were the terms of the Legislative Union made known, than that measure was speedily and thankfully accepted by the two communities.

The nature of the connection which subsisted between Great Britain and Ireland after the settlement of 1782 was unexampled. It has often been called a Federal Union. But it was not, strictly speaking, such a union. By a Federal Union is generally meant a union between two independent states unconnected before by any constitutional tie, by which union both states sacrifice something of their natural independence in exchange for the benefits expected to flow from the new connection. But Ireland was not, and for many generations had not been, in this position with respect to England. Before as after 1782 she was inextricably connected with England, and the crowns of the two kingdoms were merged or blended together.

The position of Ireland with respect to Great Britain after the settlement of 1782 was this. Her crown was inseparably annexed to that of England. This Imperial Union was not the mere result of a temporary or accidental devolution of the crowns on the same head by descent, as was the case of the Scotch and English crowns when they devolved on James I. The British and Irish crowns were irrevocably blended together. The King of England was necessarily and *ipso facto* the King of Ireland, in whatever manner he obtained the English crown. His being King of England was the *sine quâ non*, the efficient cause, of his being King of Ireland. He was King of Ireland *because* he was King of England. By the Irish statute[1] of Henry VIII, the King of England is immediately King of Ireland, and his title to the Irish crown is at once perfect, and requires no sanction from an Irish statute. Accordingly the various English Acts altering the succession of the crown in England have not been re-enacted in Ireland. When the English Parliament disposed of the English crown, they likewise disposed of the Irish crown. Thus when William III. was acknowledged as King of England in England, the Irish Parliament, by the Act of Recognition[2] admitted, that the crown of Ireland followed the grant of that of England, and that the title of the English Sovereign to be King of Ireland did not require the sanction of an Irish Act. This position has never been questioned.

There thus existed a perfect unity of the Executive in both countries; and this unity was confirmed by an Irish Act passed in 1782, during the feverish excitement of the Declaration of Independence.[3] By this Act, no Parliament could be held in Ireland without a licence under the Great Seal of Britain, and no Irish Bill could pass into law unless returned from England under the same Great Seal. As the Great Seal remains always in the possession, and under the control of the Executive of Great Britain, it is evident that this enactment accentuates the complete identity of the Executive in both countries. These considerations will be of importance

---

[1] 33 Henry VIII. c. 1.   [2] 4 Wm. and Mary, c. 1.
[3] 21 & 22 Geo. III. c. 47.

when we come to consider the conduct of the Irish Parliament in the Regency question of 1789.

But the unity between the kingdoms stopped here. The Empire was, in theory, one and indivisible, but it had two wills and two voices. It was a single head with two bodies, which occasionally showed a disposition to advance along divergent paths. The only tie which bound Great Britain and Ireland together after 1782 was the unity of the Executive. For we may leave out of account the power of refusing to place the Great Seal to an Irish Act, as the exercise of this negative would at once have placed both countries in a state of opposition.[1] The unity of the Executive may have been an adequate bond in times of repose and quietude, but the slightest sedition was sufficient to snap it. We shall see that from a few years after the adjustment of 1782, the Irish Parliament manifested alarming tendencies to separation, particularly in its refusal of a commercial treaty with Great Britain; in its illegal and unconstitutional proceedings in the Regency question in 1789; and in its policy towards the Catholics in 1793. It only requires a short consideration to perceive the dangers which threatened the Empire from the existence within it of two legislatures, leaving out of consideration altogether the hostility of the Celtic population.

The mere form of a separate Government tended to keep alive the idea of separate and antagonistic interests,

---

[1] So strongly was this felt by the English Government that they did not venture to refuse the King's assent to the Irish Act of 1793, granting the franchise to Catholics, although this favour was denied the English and Scotch Catholics for thirty years subsequently.

and weakened the conception of unity. The existence of two Parliaments led to jealousies and dissensions, and perpetually suggested the belief in every dispute, whether great or small, that something was to be gained by the one at the expense of the other, and that nothing should be mutually conceded if it could with safety be retained. But there were graver possibilities of difference which a moment of haste or anger might have called into operation.[1]

1. On a declaration of war by Great Britain, Ireland—as it was her undoubted right to discuss such a question—might have refused to take part in it, and her refusal would have paralysed the Empire. In 1791 Wolfe Tone published a pamphlet in Dublin, *An Inquiry how far Ireland is bound of right to embark in the impending Contest on the side of Great Britain*. About the same time Arthur O'Connor published an address to the electors of the county of Antrim, in which he maintained that Ireland might league herself with France or Great Britain, as one or the other alliance seemed most conducive to her interest. It will be said that these men were traitors. True; but even traitors do not address an audience unless they have reason to believe that a part at least of that audience is favourable to their views.

[1] "Within the short period of six years from the establishment of what is called the independence of the Irish Parliament—from the year 1782 to the year 1788—the foreign relations of the two countries, the commercial intercourse of the two countries, the sovereign exercise of authority in the two countries, were the subjects of litigation and dispute; and it was owing more to accident than to any other cause that they did not produce actual alienation and rupture."—Speech of Sir Robert Peel, 25th of April, 1834.

2. On a declaration, or during the continuance of a war, Ireland might have refused to grant supplies to Great Britain. "I do acknowledge," said Grattan, in the Irish Parliament, "that by your power over the purse you might dissolve the State."[1] Again, in 1800, he said, in the same place, "On these principles I suppose the dissent of Ireland on the subject of war highly improbable." By the word "improbable" he admits the possibility; and possibilities of dissent should be excluded from that unity of operation which the needs of an Empire demand.

3. She might have imposed retaliatory duties on British commodities, and provoked a commercial war of rates. This was actually proposed in the House in 1784, two years after the settlement, and was only defeated when the Commons were reminded that the Irish linen trade existed by the favour of Great Britain, and by the differential duties imposed on foreign linens.[2]

4. She might have put pressure on her Sovereign to

---

[1] *Parl. Hist.* v. 356.
[2] Pitt tells us how much this favour to Ireland cost Great Britain. "Nothing would more clearly show what would be the danger to Ireland from the competition in all its principal branches of the linen trade than the simple fact that we, even then, imported foreign linen under that heavy duty [30 per cent.] to an amount equal to a seventh part of all that Ireland was able to send us, with the preference already stated. By this arrangement alone we must be considered either as foregoing between 700,000*l.* and 800,000*l.* per annum in revenue, which we should collect if we chose to levy the same duty on all linens, Irish as well as foreign; or, on the other hand, as sacrificing perhaps at least a million sterling in the price paid for those articles by the subjects of this country."—Speech, 31st January, 1799.

declare war with a country with which Great Britain was at peace. This was not a mere possibility. At a time when Great Britain was at war with America and the whole of Western Europe, except Portugal, and when there was not a port open to her from the Baltic to the Mediterranean except Lisbon, it was proposed in the Irish Parliament to address the King, calling on him, as King of Ireland, to assert Ireland's rights by hostilities against Portugal, his only ally.[1]

5. She might have differed from Great Britain on any international question in reference to the connection between them, as she did on the Regency question.

6. She might have altered the whole scheme and theory of representation throughout the Empire, as she did in 1793, by admitting the Catholics to the franchise before a similar step was taken by Great Britain. If Grattan's proposal of admitting Catholics to Parliament had been adopted, a few months would have seen a Catholic majority in the Irish legislature.

7. She might have refused—as she did—to make a commercial treaty with Great Britain, and thus kept open the most obvious and fertile sources of mutual jealousies and discontents.

Pitt summed up in a few words the possibilities of

[1] 6th Feb. 1782.—*Parl. Reg.* i. 214; Barrington, *Rise and Fall*, pp. 94—97. Barrington's statements should never be accepted unless confirmed by other authority. He was charged in 1830 with embezzling the moneys of suitors in his court, and was removed on the petition of both Houses of Parliament. The only instance of the degradation of a judge since the tenure of the office has been "during good behaviour." His publications are full of "wonderful statements more amusing than trustworthy."

danger connected with the relation which existed between the countries before the Union. "A party in England may give to the Throne one species of advice by its Parliament. A party in Ireland may advise directly opposite upon the most essential points that involve the safety of both; upon alliance with a foreign power, for instance; upon the army; upon the navy; upon any branch of the public service; upon trade; upon commerce; or upon any point essential to the Empire at large."[1]

Grattan was fond of hurling threats, more or less concealed, against Great Britain. One of his later speeches suggests some of the many ways in which Ireland might have injured Great Britain and weakened her power and trade. "Does the minister, when he talks of an eleemosynary trade, recollect how the Irish Parliament could affect the East India Company by discontinuing the Act of 1793 granted but for a limited time? Does he recollect how she could affect the British West India monopoly by withdrawing her exclusive consumption from the British plantations? Does he recollect how we could affect the navy of England by regulations regarding our Irish provisions? Does he recollect how we could affect her Empire by forming commercial intercourse with the rest of the world?"[2]

We shall now leave the possibilities of danger and come to the actual occasions on which graver tendencies of divergence and separation were manifested by the Irish Parliament.

In 1779 Ireland obtained free trade to all the world,

[1] Cobbett's *Parl. Hist.* xxxiv. 253.   [2] 15th January, 1800.

the colonies of Great Britain only excepted.[1] A few months later the right to trade with these colonies was also given, on the single condition that Ireland should conform to such rules as Great Britain should enact for the regulation of this trade, and that her Parliament should impose on all goods imported from or exported to the colonies the same duties as Great Britain should lay on these commodities. As the colonies were the exclusive possessions of Great Britain, this concession was justly looked on as a favour, and as, to quote the words of a unanimous resolution of the Irish Commons, "a most affectionate mark of the regard and attention of Great Britain to our distresses."[2] The condition was accepted with satisfaction and gratitude, and the Irish Parliament at once enacted that all commodities imported from or exported to the colonies should be "liable to equal duties and drawbacks, and be subject to the same securities, regulations, and restrictions as the like goods are liable and subject to upon being imported from the said colonies into Great Britain, or exported thence to such colonies." On this principle of similarity of laws on the subject of trade, enactments were annually made by the Irish Parliament down to 1785. Thus in 1780 an equalising Act was passed, and in 1781 another was enacted in order that the Irish duties might correspond with new rates which Great Britain had imposed in the interval.[3] The principle was even carried

---

[1] The trade to East India, being the exclusive monopoly of a Company, was reserved. The English as well as the Irish subjects were excluded from this branch of trade.

[2] 20th Dec. 1779.—*Parl. Reg.* v. 376.   [3] *Parl. Reg.* v. 368.

further in 1782. Hitherto it had been confined to the colony trade, but the Act of this year extends to a similarity in the laws of commerce generally, and enacts that all provisions made in Great Britain conveying equal advantages and imposing equal restrictions on the inhabitants of both countries should bind the subjects in Ireland. It is remarkable that this Act was drawn by Grattan, Yelverton, and Fitzgibbon.[1] The reader will observe that at this time no objection was made by Grattan that Ireland, by adopting the rules which Great Britain should make for the regulation of the trade common to both countries, would be merely "subscribing" and "registering" laws made by Great Britain.[2] It was admitted that Ireland could not participate in the commerce of the sister kingdom without consenting to regulate that commerce by a similarity of laws. The fantastic speculation, to which the treaty of commerce in 1785 was sacrificed, had not yet been started, viz., that Ireland, by enacting the same regulations in her own Parliament under which the trade was enjoyed by Englishmen, would surrender her legislative rights.[3]

[1] *Parl. Reg.* vi. 474.
[2] Grattan's words in 1785 : " By this Bill [the proposed treaty of commerce] we are to covenant that the Parliament of Ireland shall subscribe whatever laws the Parliament of England shall prescribe ;" and—"Pass this Bill and you are not the representatives of Ireland, but the register of the British Parliament."—*Parl. Reg.* v. 355.
[3] Lord Clare asserts that this idea first arose among the Opposition in England, and that when its author " stated it to the party with whom he acted, they reprobated the deception as too gross even for Irish dupery. He told them—' I know my countrymen, and be

From 1779 to 1784 Ireland was satisfied on the subject of trade. But in the latter year it was discovered that the commercial intercourse between Great Britain and Ireland was unequal—that England poured her manufactures into Ireland and at the same time shut Ireland out from the English market by her duties. Ireland also complained of a construction which Great Britain put upon her navigation laws. At first the remedy proposed was a war of prohibitory duties, but, as we have stated, the Irish Parliament was reminded that the Irish linen trade depended on the good-will of Great Britain, and the proposal was rejected by a large majority. An address to the Crown was then proposed, and passed unanimously, praying that its servants should be directed to draw up a plan of commercial intercourse between the two countries. Accordingly such a plan was drawn up and presented to the Irish Parliament, digested into eleven resolutions. The resolutions were agreed to and sent over to England to be there re-examined and considered.

A storm of commercial jealousy arose at once in England. Petitions against the Irish proposals were laid before the British Parliament from upwards of sixty of the great cities and towns.[1] Many of the principal manufactures declared in their evidence before the House of Lords that they would remove their capital and

---

assured they will swallow the bait.'"—Lord Clare's Speech, 10th Feb. 1800. Pitt also assures us that this idea was derived from England.—Speech, 31st January, 1799.

[1] One petition alone "was signed by no less than 80,000 manufacturers of Lancashire."—Stanhope's *Pitt*, i. 269.

business to Ireland, where labour was cheaper. But Pitt was not to be moved.[1] Twenty resolutions were drawn up containing a commercial treaty between Great Britain and Ireland and passed by the English Houses of Parliament. At the same time a Bill to carry out this treaty was introduced into the British legislature, in which it was explicitly declared that the Irish Parliament was alone competent to make laws for Ireland.

These resolutions differed in number from those of Ireland, but they were practically the same. The additions referred to patents, or copyrights in books, or to regulations intended to guard against smuggling. The leading features of this treaty were: The complete opening up of the markets of both countries to each other; the equalisation of all duties between them; the relaxation of the navigation laws in favour of Ireland; the making permanent the grant to her of the colonial trade which was precarious and revocable; and the admission of Irishmen to every commercial benefit and privilege enjoyed by Englishmen. One of these resolutions,[2] the

---

[1] "It has required infinite patience, management, and exertion to meet the clamour without doors, and to prevent it infecting our supporters in the House."—Pitt to the Duke of Rutland. *Ib.* 271. The alarm among the English manufacturers was great. Mr. Peel, father of Sir Robert, actually came to Ireland, and was preparing to enter an Irish house in case the treaty should be made.— Speech of the Right Hon. John Beresford, 19th March, 1800.

[2] "4. That it is highly important to the general interests of the British Empire that the laws for regulating trade and navigation should be the same in Great Britain and Ireland, and therefore that it is essential towards carrying into effect the present settlement that all laws which have been made or shall be made in Great Britain for securing exclusive privileges to the ships and mariners

fourth, contained the same principle of similarity in the laws of trade and navigation which had been regularly adopted in the Acts passed in the Irish Parliament since 1779, and stood recorded in its proceedings. It was this resolution which fired the petulant jealousy of the Irish Parliament, though the provisions of this resolution were already the law of Ireland as established by the Act of 1782, which Act had been drawn up by Grattan, Yelverton and Fitzgibbon.

The resolutions, after they had been agreed to by the English Parliament, were sent over to Ireland. They were there digested into a Bill by Mr. Orde, the Secretary of the Lord-Lieutenant, and in this shape presented to the Irish Commons. The Bill was received with an Irish howl. Ireland was determined to resent an offence that never was intended, and to repel an injury that never was offered. Though in every session since 1779, when she obtained the colony trade, she had in her Acts recited the condition on which she held it, and re-enacted the British rates after reciting them; though the principle of re-enacting such regulations as Great Britain had made or should make for the regulation of trade and navigation was recorded in her own Act;[1] though the British Houses had just declared in a joint address to the Crown that the Irish Parliament was alone competent to

of Great Britain, Ireland, and the British colonies, and for regulating and restraining the trade of the British colonies and plantations, such laws imposing the same restraints and conferring the same benefits on the subjects of both kingdoms, should be in force in Ireland by laws to be passed by the Parliament of that kingdom for the same time and in the same manner as in Great Britain."

[1] 21 & 22 Geo. III. c. 48, 1781-2.

make laws for Ireland, and the British Bill repeated this declaration; and though, what is strangest of all, it was specially provided in the Bill that the treaty should not bind Ireland a moment longer than she pleased,[1] it was rejected on the imaginary ground that it threatened the legislative independence of Ireland.

Grattan was told in the House that his objections to the treaty were entirely "void of foundation, and fraught with absurdity and mischief—calculated to answer the worst of purposes, to spread a false alarm through all parts of the kingdom, to irritate the public without just cause against the British Parliament, and to persuade the people that the constitutional independence of their country was in danger at the very moment that it was most secure, at the very moment that all branches of the legislature in both countries were vying with each other which of them should assert the independence of Ireland in the strongest terms."[2] He was warned in the same place that his doctrine and words led to separation.[3] But Grattan was as obstinate as he was impervious to argument. With the fanatical cry of "Perish the

---

[1] Grattan admitted this: "It is declared by the Bill that the King, Lords, and Commons of Great Britain must pronounce by a positive statute that Ireland has broken the treaty before she can be charged with a breach of it. But if Ireland thinks that Great Britain has violated it, no other authority is thought necessary for charging the breach upon her but an address of both Houses of the Irish Parliament. This is a strong guard to Ireland against the influence that ministers may be supposed to have over it, and consequently an advantage on the part of Ireland."—Grattan's Speech, *Parl. Reg.* v. 366.

[2] *Ib.* 367.   [3] *Ib.* 417.

Empire, live the Constitution,"[1] he threw away what would have been of inestimable advantage to his country. The tariff between England and Ireland, the Channel trade, and the navigation laws remained unsettled, and a Legislative Union loomed into sight.

Grattan affected to believe that the acceptance of the treaty by Ireland would have been a subversion of her legislative independence. Charles James Fox took a very different view of the position which Ireland would occupy. Here are his words: "The whole tendencies of the proposals appeared to him to go the length of appointing Ireland the sole guardian of the laws of navigation, and grand arbitress of all the commercial interests of the Empire."[2] Foster, the Chancellor of the Irish Exchequer, urged in vain "if Great Britain grants us a full partnership in all her trade in all her colonies; if she admits us to a full participation in the benefits of her navigation laws, by which she has raised herself to be the greatest commercial power in the world; if she does not call upon us to contribute to the expense of the partnership, but merely to receive our share of the profits; and says we may continue in that partnership only so long as we choose, can any man say the condition of it is a surrender of our legislature? Let us then look at the subject free from imaginary dread of constitution."[3]

When we remember that the Scotch Union was long retarded by Scotland's insisting upon having the benefits of trading with the English colonies, and of the navigation laws, favours which England refused; and

---

[1] Grattan's words, *Parl. Reg.* v. 356.
[2] Cobbett's *Parl. Hist.* xxv. 333.   [3] *Parl. Reg.* v. 412.

that the Scotch required an express provision for that purpose[1] to be inserted in the Act of Union, we cannot sufficiently wonder at the caprice of Ireland in refusing what was freely and generously offered at her own suggestion, and with a view only of a union of common interests and affection. Equal laws and regulations of trade were gladly accepted by Scotland, they were refused by Ireland in a tempest of indignation.

It was not for want of advice that Ireland made the mistake of rejecting the commercial treaty. We shall only quote the counsels of two of her friends, the one from the greatness of him who gave it, the other from the position then and afterwards filled by its author. On the 25th May, 1785, Edmund Burke wrote to a friend of Grattan's while these proceedings were going on :[2] "This is the only moment, in my idea, for Ireland to fix her happiness, commercial and political, upon a solid and firm basis. If pertinacity or an ill-understood punctilio should be suffered to step in, to prevent the operation of the good sense of your country, and prevent our now coming to a final settlement upon some system that may connect the two countries permanently, and for ever lay asleep every motive of jealousy and dispute, every man either of wisdom or feeling will soon have reason to regret the day when the question was first stirred amongst us, and that anything was done to let

---

[1] See Act of Scotch Union, Defoe, *History of the Union*.

[2] The letter was evidently intended to be shown to Grattan. It was found among his papers, and is quoted by his son. *Grattan's Life*, iii. 252.

all *loose from the bands of the old situation*,[1] before due consideration was had upon what should be those of the new."

The other is that of Mr. Foster, the Chancellor of the Irish Exchequer, and afterwards Speaker, and the recognised leader of the Anti-Unionists. He regarded the refusal of the treaty as leading directly to separation. The statement is weighty, even solemn, and every word falls on the ear like the stroke of a bell. "I could run on for hours into the many benefits of this system, but I have tired the House too long; let me only implore you not to reject the measure for ill-founded visionary objections, or sacrifice realities to shadows. If this infatuated country gives up the present offer she may look for it again in vain. Things cannot remain as they are, commercial jealousy is roused. It will increase with two independent legislatures, if they do not mutually declare the principles whereby their powers shall be separately employed in directing the common concerns of trade; and without a united interest of commerce in a commercial empire, political union will receive many shocks, and separation of interests must threaten separation of connection which every honest Irishman must shudder 'to look at. I will say that if this measure be refused, Ireland will receive more solid injury than from any other evil that ever befel her. It is in vain for gentlemen to think we can go on as we have done for some years, or to expect to cope with England in a destructive war of bounties. Our situation must every day

[1] The italics are in the letter as given in *Grattan's Life*.

become more difficult, and it is impossible to foresee the event."[1]

Three days afterwards he renewed his entreaty to the House. "I will stand or fall with the Bill, that not a line in it touches your constitution. It is now left to the decision of the country, it is not abandoned,[2] God forbid it should, and I trust I shall see the country ask it at our hands. That we may be able to obtain it, shall be my prayer, and it will be my pride at a future day, when its real value shall be known, that I bore a leading share in this transaction; that I laboured to procure for Ireland solid and substantial benefits which even two years ago no man had an idea of ever looking to."

Had this treaty been accepted, it would have poured a current of wealth into Ireland. Commercial intercourse would have smoothed all asperities existing between the two countries, and done away with mutual jealousies and discontents. A constant and uninterrupted communication would have drawn them closer, and united them in the bonds of common interests and affection. And Ireland might have again renewed the offer which she made in 1703 and 1707, and asked for, what her coming difficulties made necessary, an incorporate union with Great Britain.

Four years later another Imperial question arose—that of the Regency.

On the 5th of February, 1789, the malady of the

[1] *Parl. Reg.* v. 413.
[2] Unhappily, owing to the violent opposition it met with, it was abandoned.

King was announced to the Irish Parliament in the Speech from the Throne. On the following day, documents explaining the nature and extent of the King's illness were laid on the table of the House of Commons,[1] and it was proposed that an interval of ten days—that is, to the 16th—should be allowed for the consideration of this momentous question. Grattan moved an amendment that the House should sit on the 11th, and this amendment was carried. On the 11th, when the House met, Fitzgibbon pressed for "some decent space of time for deliberation." But Grattan was inexorable, and the House, without a tittle of evidence before them of the then health of the King, for the documents which had been laid on their table were two months old, came to two resolutions. The first was "that the personal exercise of the Royal authority was interrupted for the present by His Majesty's indisposition." The other was "that an humble address should be presented to His Royal Highness the Prince of Wales to request of him to take upon himself the government of this kingdom during His Majesty's indisposition, under the style and title of Prince Regent of Ireland." As a matter of fact the King was declared convalescent in the *London Gazette* of the 11th, the very day on which the Irish Commons suspended him from his royal functions. The Committee of the House made their report on the same night, and it was instantly agreed to. The next day, the 12th, the Address was voted, and sent up to the Lords for their concurrence. Thus, within six days from

[1] Copies of the examinations and reports of the King's physicians taken before Committees of the British Parliament.

the time when this matter had been submitted to the Commons, did they dispose of it without a semblance of deliberation, and, as we shall show, in direct violation of the law, for they had no power whatever to appoint a Regent of Ireland. On the 18th, both Houses waited on the Lord-Lieutenant, and requested him to transmit the Address to the Prince of Wales. The Lord-Lieutenant declined to do so, informing them "that under the impressions which he felt of public duty, and of the oath of office he had taken, he was obliged to decline transmitting their Address into Great Britain, not conceiving himself warranted to lay before the Prince of Wales an Address purporting to invest his Royal Highness with powers to take upon him the government of this realm before he shall, by law, be enabled to do so." The Commons fired up at this refusal, which they treated as an insult, and voted a censure on the Lord-Lieutenant. As this nobleman had declined to forward the Address, Commissioners were chosen to proceed to London and present it to the Prince of Wales. On their arrival in that city, the Commissioners found the King restored to health.[1]

On the 20th of February, the same day on which the Commissioners who were to carry the Address to London were appointed, the Commons, at Grattan's suggestion, placed the following resolution on their records: "That in addressing His Royal Highness the Prince of Wales to take upon himself the government

---

[1] The Commissioners presented the Address on the 26th February. The Prince acquainted them with the happy change in the King's health, and dismissed them with thanks.

of this country on the behalf, and in the name of His Majesty, during His Majesty's present indisposition and no longer, the Lords and Commons of Ireland *have exercised an undoubted right and discharged an indispensable duty, to which in the present emergency they alone are competent.*" These are the facts of the case; we may now consider its constitutional aspects and the illegality and dangers of these proceedings.

We have seen that perfect unity of the Executive in England and Ireland was established by the fundamental laws of the connection, that by the Irish Act of Henry VIII., the Executive of England, if King in England, was *ipso facto* the Executive of Ireland, and that the powers of such Executive were derived only and solely from his being appointed in England. Though the word Regent was not mentioned in this Act, its spirit and provision included such an officer. As Fitzgibbon[1] told the House, "it is not the mere name of King, it is not the ring of gold that encircles the monarch's head, which is the object of this law. No! The object of the law is that the chief executive magistrate and the chief executive power in both countries should be one and the same." If any doubt as to the construction of this Act remained, it was removed by the later Irish Acts of William and Mary, and the Act of 1782. The Act of William and Mary declared that the crown of Ireland and all the powers and prerogatives belonging to it should

---

[1] Every reader of the Irish debates must be struck by the directness with which this distinguished man goes to the kernel of every question. A clearer head there was not in Ireland.

be for ever annexed to and dependent on the crown of England. The Act of 1782 made the Great Seal of Great Britain necessary to the summoning of an Irish Parliament and the passing of Irish Acts. "It is clear," says the leader of the Anti-Unionists in 1799, "that the Act annexing the crown of Henry VIII. extends to the person authorised by Britain to administer regal power, whether King, Queen, or Regent. Our law of 1782 concerning the Great Seal puts it out of doubt; whoever is Regent of Great Britain has that great Seal; the functions of the Irish legislature must cease without its use, and therefore the Regent of Britain alone can represent the third estate of the Irish legislature."[1]

If then, the British Regent was necessarily and *ipso facto* the Regent of Ireland, and if his Irish powers and prerogatives were only derived from his prior appointment in Great Britain, the Irish Parliament by appointing an Irish Regent, and by recording and claiming that they were alone competent to do so, acted in direct violation of the laws regulating the connection between the two kingdoms. Their declaration that they had the power of "choosing"[2] endangered the only bond which existed between England and Ireland—viz., the necessary and perpetual identity of the Executive, which excluded all power of choice.

To nominate a Regent for Ireland before his appointment in Great Britain was illegal and unconstitutional;

---

[1] The Speaker, 11th April, 1799.
[2] "By the determination of the Irish Parliament in choosing for their Regent," &c.—Grattan's words, 15th Jan., 1800.

to do so afterwards would have been superfluous, as by his British appointment he would have been immediately and *ipso facto* Regent of Ireland. The proper conduct to have been observed by the Irish Parliament was, to have waited till a Regent had been appointed in Great Britain, and then to have passed an Act of Recognition, as was done in the case of William III.

By nominating a Regent for Ireland, before he was appointed in Great Britain, the Irish Parliament presented to the British Parliament the dangerous alternative of accepting the Irish Regent as British Regent, and thereby surrendering their own right of appointing, or of setting aside the Irish nominee, and compelling obedience in Ireland to the person appointed by the British Parliament. This would have been but little short of war.

By nominating the Prince of Wales as Regent of Ireland, before his appointment in Great Britain, the Irish Parliament not only usurped a right of election which the Constitution did not give them, but they ran the risk of appointing a different Regent from the person named by the British Parliament. The Prince of Wales might have refused the office on the limited terms offered. He might not even have been Regent at all, for the Queen might have been appointed. If this had taken place, the Governments of the two countries would have been entirely different. The three estates in each country would have been full, though completely separate. In Great Britain there would have been the Lords and Commons with a Regent appointed by the British

Parliament. In Ireland there would have been the Irish Lords and Commons with a Regent appointed by them.

The Address of the Irish Parliament to the Prince of Wales gave him full regal powers.[1] It was the intention of the British Parliament to grant him the Regency with limited authority.[2] The unity of the Executive in both countries clearly demands that its prerogatives and powers should be the same in England and Ireland. It may be even asserted that the Irish Parliament, by intrusting their nominee with different powers from those given by the British Parliament, would have appointed a different Regent from the one to be named in Great Britain. The Executive has no bodily outline or conformation. It is only known to the other estates by the powers, capacities and limitations with which it is endowed. It is not a question of individuality, but of a creation of the law. A difference of powers constitutes a different executive, for its unity does not depend upon the sameness of the person filling it, but on the identity of the prerogatives exercised by him.

The principal offence of the Irish Parliament against

---

[1] The Irish Address conferred on the Regent "all regal powers, jurisdiction, and prerogatives to the Crown and Government belonging." "Our method," says Grattan, "differs also from that pursued by Great Britain, inasmuch as we give the full exercise of the regal power."—*Parl. Reg.* ix. 38.

[2] The Prince had consented to receive the Regency subject to three limitations—1. The care of the King's person, household, and the appointment of officers and servants was reserved to the Queen. 2. The Regent was not to be empowered to dispose of the real or personal property of the King, or to grant any office in reversion, or any pension or office except during pleasure, or 3. to bestow any peerage except on the King's issue.—May, *Const. Hist.* i. 153, 154.

the Constitution, was the attempt of choosing a Regent. They had no choice or right of choice. They were bound by their own laws to follow the choice of Great Britain of an Executive, and such Executive when chosen by Great Britain became, at once and without Irish sanction, that of Ireland. The precedent of choosing by an Irish Parliament would have been most dangerous to the connection, and would have led them far astray. Let us suppose that it was not a question of the King's inability, but of a failure of issue in the Brunswick line. Can it be doubted that the Irish Parliament, which rushed precipitately to decide the Regency question before the British Parliament had time to come to a solution, would have greedily seized on such an opportunity of showing its legislative independence?

A short conversation in the Irish Commons will show the incredible levity with which Grattan treated this Imperial question:

"Mr. Hobart asked, were the Irish Commissioners immediately on their arrival in London to present the address to His Royal Highness, even though he were not yet invested with the Regency in England? Or were they to wait till such investiture should take place?

"Mr. Grattam said, 'That difficulty will be removed, for I think His Royal Highness will be invested before the Commissioners can arrive.'

"Mr. Hobart: 'I beg leave to say that I am not answered, for my question supposes the Commissioners may possibly arrive before His Royal Highness is invested with the Regency.'"

No answer was given, for Grattan was desirous of anticipating the action of the British Parliament.

The commercial treaty and the Regency dispute referred to the connection between the two countries, and was in some degree external, but the internal legislation of Ireland also threatened the bond which kept the kingdoms together. In 1793 an Irish Act admitted Catholic forty-shilling freeholders to the franchise, while it reserved the right of sitting in Parliament to Protestants.[1] At one stroke the Irish electorate was tripled, and a peasantry of whose ignorance, poverty and superstition, we can form a very inadequate idea, and many of whom did not speak English, were at once given the power of determining every county election. Happily for the peace of the country, for otherwise the whole representation would have been in their possession, the pocket-boroughs were Protestant, the Catholics being excluded from them in practice, though not by law. In Ireland almost all the land was let on lives,[2] and the practical effect of the Act was to create something like universal suffrage.[3] Tenants whose rent did not exceed half-a-crown were admitted to the franchise.[4] This Act of the Irish Parliament

[1] This was the most illogical measure ever passed by a legislature. The law said to the Catholics, "You may vote, but you must not vote for those you have confidence in. You must vote for those who are opposed to your claims and of whose principles you disapprove."

[2] Wakefield's *Ireland*, ii. 300. *Parl. Hist.* xiii. 213.

[3] Wakefield, ii. 301.

[4] "I have known freeholders registered among mountain tenantry whose yearly head rent did not exceed 2s. 6d., but, living upon this half-crown tenure, were enabled to swear to a derivative interest of 40s. per annum."—Wakefield, ii. 301.

altered the whole scheme and theory of representation in the Empire, and destroyed its equality and conformity throughout the three kingdoms. The Catholic question was not peculiar to Ireland; there were many of that body in England, and the highlands of Scotland were then largely Catholic. The relation of these citizens to the Sovereign of the Empire was an Imperial question, and should not have been precipitated or hurried forward in any part of the dominion without the concurrence and counsel of the Central Executive. Though the Irish Parliament did not trouble themselves to maintain conformity in the laws relating to Catholics throughout the Empire, they ought at least to have hesitated before passing a suicidal Act, which at the same time threatened the connection with England and their own existence as a Protestant legislature. For the admission of the Irish Catholics to the franchise would have given them before many years, if the Union had not intervened, a majority in this assembly, and made the Parliament of Ireland Catholic. It is vain to say that the denial of the right of sitting would have long delayed this consummation. The admission to the elective franchise does draw with it, though not immediately, the right of sitting; for how can it be urged that men are fit to elect and unfit to be elected? The reservation of the right of sitting would have been done away with, nor are the steps in the progress hard to be discerned. The Catholics would not long have wanted representatives to help them to effect this. There were many nominal Protestants in Ireland, and many adventurers among the Protestants themselves, such as Tone and Russell, who would have offered to take the side of the Catholics, and obey their instructions. The counties would at once have been taken possession of, and with the county representation in the hands of that body, and its growing preponderance in the larger constituencies, the cities and towns would soon have followed the example of the counties. There would have been a bitter contest for the private or pocket-boroughs, for the Protestants would not have easily yielded up the last defences of their constitution and establishment. But the final result cannot be doubted, and the right of sitting in Parliament would have been extorted. The whole, or an immense majority of the representatives would then have been Catholic, and the legislative bodies in Great Britain and Ireland would have been differently constituted.

There would then have been a Catholic Ireland united by a single tie, that of the Executive, to a Protestant Great Britain, whose Protestant monarch was bound by his coronation oath, as his Parliament was bound by theirs, to maintain the Protestant establishment and religion. The Catholics were attached to their own religion, and naturally adverse to a Protestant establishment. They could not be expected to be friendly to a constitution which was founded on that establishment. Dissensions, essential differences on fundamental questions, must have arisen between the two countries, and the single tie must soon have been worn away.

Dissensions would have arisen even if the Catholics had been prudent and moderate. But political prudence and moderation are not to be expected from a community without any constitutional experience or training. The Catholics, founding their claims on what they observed in England, might have demanded a Catholic establishment and Catholic ascendency. They might, and probably would, have demanded the repeal of the Act of Settlement and the restoration of the forfeited lands. If they had done so, civil war could not have been avoided, and a rebellion, supported not by a part of the body as in 1798, but by the whole united force of the Catholics of Ireland, would have taxed the power of Great Britain, encumbered as she then was, to subdue it.

Not content with the admission of the Catholics to the franchise, Grattan proposed a further scheme in 1797, on the eve of the rebellion.[1] By this scheme Catholics were to be admitted to Parliament, and to all the great offices of State, in the same way as Protestants, and Ireland was to be divided, after the French model, into departments, each consisting of 5,000 houses, and returning two representatives, elected, not by freeholders, but by householders. By the side of the new arrangement the old county representation and qualification were to remain as they were. This system would have abolished the right of every city, town, and borough in Ireland, as such, to return representatives, and would have at once made the Parliament and Government of the country almost exclusively Catholic. We can only speculate on the mischief and danger which this plan, if it had been adopted, would have caused to

[1] It was Grattan's, though introduced by his friend, W. B. Ponsonby.— See a letter to Grattan, his *Life*, by his son, iv. 409.

the Empire, for Parliament recoiled from further concession, and the bill was rejected by one hundred and seventy votes to thirty.

This was the final blow to Grattan's waning authority, and all confidence in him was lost.[1] As his influence declined, his jealousy of the English connection degenerated into positive hostility, and his Irish career, which had opened with such splendour in 1782, ended in general distrust and suspicion.[2] On the rejection of his last proposal he seceded from Parliament and did not re-appear in it until his pre-arranged and theatrical entrance on the night of the 15th of January, 1800, when he delivered the first of his anti-Union speeches.[3] His later Irish speeches and writings, for his tone was moderate and guarded in the British House of Commons, are the fertile sources of all the denunciations and invectives against England with which we have since become well acquainted. Nor should it ever be forgotten that he was the author and expounder of the meanest political doctrine ever preached to man, viz., that England's necessity is Ireland's opportunity; a doctrine totally inconsistent

---

[1] From 1794 his followers in the House never exceeded thirty, sometimes falling to fourteen, and even seven.

[2] His name was erased from their list of freeholders by the Corporations of Dublin and Derry, and by that of the Guild of Merchants in Dublin. His portrait was taken down from the walls of the University, and he was dismissed the Privy Council.—*Grattan's Life*, iv. 407.

[3] He entered the House supported by W. B. Ponsonby and Arthur Moore. At this time he was not yet fifty-four years of age, and he survived the Union twenty years.

with any loyalty to the connection between the two countries.[1]

The truth is, the real Grattan is forgotten or unknown. A glorified figure, labelled with his name, stalks across the stage of Irish history and distracts our attention. To the orator, to the mere master of expression, the nobler title of statesman has been awarded by the superstition of a noisy and ignorant multitude.

[1] "To maintain which (free trade) Ireland must continue in a state of armed preparation, dreading the approach of a general peace, and attributing all she holds dear to the calamitous condition of the British interest in every quarter of the globe."—19th April, 1780. "The American war was the Irish harvest; from that period, as from the lucky moment of your fate your commerce, constitution, and mind took form and vigour."—12th Aug. 1785.

CHAPTER IV.

Union Debates in the Irish Parliament, 1799.

RUMOURS of a Legislative Union had long been current in Ireland before the year 1799. We have seen that even so far back as 1698 Molyneux longed for such an incorporation, but thought it a happiness which was not likely to fall to the lot of Ireland. In default of such a fortunate issue, he devoted himself to work out the legislative independence of his country.

The Scotch Union appears to have affected powerfully the minds of leading Irishmen, and, from the time of this occurrence the idea of a union with Great Britain began to ripen and gather volume. We have seen that the Irish Parliament in 1703, and, again, about the time of the Scotch Union in 1707, desired and proposed a legislative incorporation with the Parliament of England, and all through the eighteenth century a long line of distinguished Irishmen joined English thinkers and writers in recommending such a measure. In the early part of it, even Swift[1] thought that a union with Great Britain would be a gain to Ireland. But it was not till after the settlement of 1782 that the idea of a union

[1] See his tale, or parable, of *The Injured Lady*.

became more general. Some then thought that the concession of Irish Independence in that year without any international compact or treaty, whether political or commercial, to serve as the means of keeping the two countries united, rendered a Legislative Union indispensable.[1] The subsequent conduct of the Irish Parliament on the Regency question,[2] the unsettled state of the connection with Great Britain, and the rebellion had alarmed many. Ireland had suffered greatly from the violence and cruelty of both parties during the disturbances of 1798. Among thoughtful men a vague feeling of unrest prevailed, and a belief was spread that something was wanting to restore peace and quiet, and to put an end to the dissensions which troubled the country.

But among the Catholics there was no doubt, for they had made up their minds that the salvation of Ireland could be wrought out only through a union with Great Britain.[3] They were well aware that emancipation would not be granted willingly by a Protestant Irish Parliament, and that it could only be allowed, if ever, at the expense of civil dissensions, and after a long contest. The declarations of the Catholics in favour of a union, harp on the idea that that measure alone would remove the baneful spirit of intolerance and

---

[1] See a remarkable letter, *Cast. Corr.* i. 436.

[2] Lord Downshire, a strong opponent of the Union in 1800, was of opinion that the English Ministry should have introduced a Union in 1789.

[3] See the letters and opinions of the Catholic Archbishops of Dublin and Tuam, of the Bishop of Cork, Dr. Bodkin, and others, quoted in Chapter VI.

religious animosity.¹ The clergy and the laity of that body both looked forward to the Union as the means of obtaining emancipation, and putting an end to Protestant ascendency. But there was a third consideration which affected the minds of their clergy especially, and that was, they were thoroughly alarmed at the spread of French or republican sentiments and principles in Ireland. They knew well of the treatment which the Pope and their religion had received at the hands of the French army, and of the manner in which their churches had been despoiled in every country where the republican arms had prevailed. They had witnessed how the apostles of liberty, under the name of contributions, had pillaged or profaned every building which was set apart for the worship of God or the performance of sacred duties by men and women who had devoted themselves to his service. To use the words of the Catholic Bishop, afterwards Archbishop Dillon : " they saw the Supreme Pastor of their Church not only reviled and calumniated, but also stripped of that property which enabled him to display a generosity and benevolence worthy of his high station, and to propagate the gospel of Christ amongst the most remote nations of the globe."² And at the same time they saw England

---

¹ See the declarations of the Catholics of Waterford, *Belfast News Letter*, 23rd Aug. 1799; of those of Cork, *ib.*; of those of the baronies of Tirawley, &c., *ib.*; of Kilkenny, *ib.* 13th Sept.; of Tipperary and Cahir, *ib.*, 3rd Sep. ; of Wexford, *ib.*, 19th Nov.; of Dundalk, *ib*, 15th Oct. ; of New Ross, *ib.*, 29th Oct.

² Address of Edward Dillon, Bishop of Kilmacduagh and Kilenora, to the Catholic laity of said dioceses, 6th April, 1798.—*Cast.*

taking the part and acting as the protector of the Holy
See. This consideration, joined to the others which we
have mentioned, affected them powerfully. Accordingly
they set themselves to oppose the further spreading of
French principles and the teachings of the United Irishmen among their flocks. As the principal objects of
the United Irishmen were to effect a separation from
Great Britain, and a union with France, the Catholic
clergy threw their weight into the opposite scale, and
gave their whole support to an incorporation of their
country with Great Britain.

On the other hand, the idea of a Legislative Union was
to the majority of the Protestants distasteful. The lower
orders among them were disposed to hostility to the
measure by an apprehension that it would put an
end to their political superiority, and reduce them to
an equality with their Catholic fellow subjects. But
the higher classes were influenced by nobler impulses
and motives. To them the Union, at the first mention
of it, and before its terms were made known, wore the
appearance, not of an equal alliance with Great Britain,
but of submission to a more powerful neighbour. The
splendour and prestige of national independence blinded
their eyes and prejudiced them against a cool consideration of the advantages of the proposal. The fear, too,
that if Ireland were united to the more powerful
kingdom, her interests would be neglected, exercised
a strong influence on the minds of many.[1] Their

Corr. i. 172. This prelate was appointed Archbishop of Tuam
in 1799.

[1] It was this fear which, as he tells us, influenced Plunket.

patriotism was alarmed, and they dreaded the measure as entailing injury to their country. These feelings were natural and laudable, but they diminished in strength as it became known that the conditions of Union were such as Ireland could accept without loss of her national dignity. Opposition to the measure was also weakened by the division of opinion which prevailed among those who were in favour of the legislative independence of Ireland. One party, hostile to the full emancipation of the Catholics, believed that they could maintain the independence of the country and, at the same time, retain disqualifying laws and Protestant ascendency. The other thought it was necessary to admit the Catholics to a full participation in the rights of citizenship, but this party saw no danger to their Church, their Protestant constitution, and the British connection, in the admission to Parliament of a body which was certainly opposed to the two former. It is evident that the policy of both parties was fraught with danger, and that the blindness of one was only equalled by the quixotic confidence of the other. It was impossible to preserve the independence of Ireland and to retain at the same time disqualifying laws. It was equally impossible to open Parliament to the Catholics without disturbing the fundamental principles of the Irish Constitution, and endangering the connection with Great Britain. There remained a *tertium quid*, viz., a Union, which would secure for ever Ireland's real legislative independence, and would make the emancipation of the Catholics feasible and safe.

Such was the state of feeling in Ireland on this

question, when in the spring of the year, 1798, a pamphlet[1] was published by Mr. Edward Cooke, the Under Secretary, recommending a Legislative Union between Great Britain and Ireland. So great was the interest excited by this publication that it reached a ninth edition before the end of the year, and as many as thirty pamphlets, some in favour of a Union, but the majority against it, appeared before the 1st of January, 1799.[2] The excitement was not limited to a war of words. On the 9th of December, a meeting of the Bar was convened to deliberate on the question of a Legislative Union, and a resolution was carried, by a large majority, to the effect that the proposal of such a measure was "an innovation highly dangerous and improper at the present juncture of the country." On the 17th of the same month a meeting of the Dublin Corporation and citizens, and on the following day one of the bankers and merchants of Dublin were held on the subject. At both it was unanimously agreed to oppose any proposal of a Union. About the same time Trinity College, and the gentry and freeholders of the county of Dublin held meetings respectively, and protested against a Union. The freeholders of the county of Westmeath likewise declared against such a measure.

The Parliament met on the 22nd of January, 1799, Lord Cornwallis in his speech after alluding to the attempts which had been lately made to separate the

[1] Its title was, *Arguments for and against a Union between Great Britain and Ireland.*

[2] More than a hundred pamphlets on the Union still exist.

two kingdoms recommended to the particular consideration of the two Houses the most effectual means of consolidating into one firm and lasting fabric the strength, power, and resources of the British Empire."[1]

In the Peers, Lord Glandore moved an address to the King which adopted the words of the Viceroy's speech, and in which the House undertook to give "their fullest attention to the consideration of the most effectual means of improving a connection which was essential to the common security of both kingdoms, and of consolidating into one firm and lasting fabric the power and resources of the British Empire."

Lord Powerscourt moved an amendment which, while it expressed the wish of the House for a continuance of the connection with Great Britain, and a strong desire of improving it consistently with the freedom and independence of Ireland, intimated a doubt of the competence of Parliament to effectuate an Incorporative Union.

Lord Bellamont was in favour of the amendment except that portion which called in question the competence of Parliament. He requested the mover to

[1] This paragraph of the speech was as follows:—"The unremitting industry with which our enemies persevere in their avowed designs of endeavouring to effect a separation of this kingdom from Great Britain must have engaged your particular attention; and His Majesty commands me to express his anxious hope that this consideration, joined to the sentiment of mutual affection and common interest, may dispose the Parliaments in both kingdoms to provide the most effectual means of maintaining and improving a connection essential to their common security, and of consolidating as far as possible into one firm and lasting fabric the strength, the power, and the resources of the British Empire."

withdraw that part. Lord Powerscourt was willing to do so, but the House would not allow him, as it was considered necessary to clear away all doubts as to the competence of Parliament. On a motion being made for leave to withdraw, a discussion arose and it was refused by forty-six votes to nineteen.

Lord Bellamont, omitting the point of competence, then moved two amendments; first, to expunge the words "and of consolidating as far as possible, into one firm and lasting fabric the strength, power, and resources of the British Empire." This amendment was negatived. He then moved that the following words should be inserted: "so far as may be consistent with the permanent enjoyment, exercise, and tutelary vigilance of our resident and independent Parliament as established, acknowledged and recognised." This amendment produced a debate, and this motion was also negatived. The question was then put on the original address, and it was carried by fifty-two votes to seventeen, a majority of thirty-five for Government. A general disposition to take into their consideration the question of a Union was thus shown to be entertained by two-thirds of the House. Fourteen of the minority protested.[1] The principal speakers were, for the Government, Lords Clare, Carleton, and Yelverton; for the Opposition, Lords Powerscourt, Bellamont, and Farnham.

It is remarkable that though the Irish Peerage then con-

[1] Leinster, Granard, Belvedere, Arran, Mountcashel, Charlemont (Volunteer Charlemont), Bellamont, Kilkenny, Belmore, Powerscourt, De Vesci, William Down and Connor, Dunsaney, Lismore.

sisted of about 210 members, forty of whom were entirely unconnected with Ireland, not one voted in the majority on this occasion who was not interested in the country, either as a large landholder, law lord, or prelate.

On the same day a similar address was moved in the Commons by Lord Tyrone. This member and his seconder asked the House merely to give the great and important matter which occupied the public mind, and was recommended by their Sovereign, a full and free consideration without pledging themselves to its support.

Sir John Parnell said that although the question of a union was not specifically mentioned in the address, nor directly recommended to the House, it was necessary to "oppose it *in limine*" as being a simple question and not requiring any further discussion or information. He then entered upon a general argument against the principle of a Union.

Lord Castlereagh was bound to say that although there was not any specific pledge to the measure in the address, yet it was clearly implied. He had no difficulty in saying that the only means of settling the country in tranquillity and permanent connection with Great Britain were to be found in a Legislative Union. He intended at an early day to submit a special motion to the House.

Mr. George Ponsonby argued that Parliament was incompetent to subvert the Constitution. He then considered the probable effects of the measure on the prosperity of the nation; and after appealing to the House to support Irish independence, he moved an amendment that the following words should be inserted in the address: "But maintaining the undoubted birthright of the people of Ireland to have a free and independent legislature resident within that kingdom, as it was asserted by the Parliament of this kingdom in 1782, and acknowledged and ratified by His Majesty and the Parliament of Great Britain upon the final adjustment of the discontents and jealousies then prevailing among His Majesty's loyal subjects of this country."

A general debate of unprecedented length followed. It continued without intermission from four o'clock on Tuesday to one o'clock p.m. of the next day, an interval of twenty hours. Thirty spoke for, and forty-five against the Government. Excluding the Speaker and tellers, 212 members divided. The contest was so close that the amendment was lost by a majority of one only,[1] 105 voting for it, and 106 against it. When the amendment was negatived, the question was put for agreeing to the address as it had stood originally. This was carried by 107 to 105, a majority of two for the Government.

The principal speakers were: for the Government, Lord Castlereagh, Mr. Corry (the Chancellor of the Exchequer), the Law Officers, Mr., afterwards Sir William, Smith, Sir John Blaquiere, Mr. Conolly, and Mr. McNaghten. Against, Sir Lawrence Parsons, George Ponsonby, Mr., afterwards Sir Jonah, Barrington, George Ogle, and Mr., afterwards Lord, Plunket.

The tone of the anti-Unionists in this debate was decidedly violent, even warlike. Many of them more

---

[1] The second reading of the first Reform Bill was carried by a majority of one, and that was a defection.

than hinted at the *ultima ratio*, the sword. Plunket told the House that, if they passed an Act of Union, it would be a mere nullity, and no man would be bound to obey it. J. M. O'Donnell said, "I will oppose it in the field. I have made up my mind on my conduct. I shall live free or fall by cut six of some Hessian sabre, or some other foreign mercenary." Another O'Donnell, eldest son of Sir Neil O'Donnell, and Colonel of the Mayo Regiment, declared that, if the Union was carried, he should consider himself discharged from his allegiance, and that he should take the field at the head of his regiment to oppose the Union, and "to resist rebels in rich clothes with as much energy as he had ever resisted rebels in rags." For this speech Colonel O'Donnell was dismissed his regiment.[1]

It was during this debate that Plunket made use of the words with which Cobbett afterwards used to twit him. "For my own part, I will resist it to the last gasp of my existence and with the last drop of my blood; and, when I feel the hour of my dissolution approaching, I will, like the father of Hannibal, take my children to the altar and swear them to eternal hostility against the invaders of their country's freedom."[2]

[1] This gentleman died before the meeting of Parliament in 1800.
[2] It is interesting to compare Plunket's sentiments as expressed in this speech with those which he afterwards entertained when his judgment was matured. "As an Irishman I opposed that Union; as an Irishman I avow that I did so openly and boldly, nor am I now ashamed of what I then did. But though in my resistance to it I had been prepared to go the length of any man, I am now equally prepared to do all in my power to render it close and indissoluble. One of the apprehensions on which my opposition was

The tactics and the conduct of the Opposition deserve our attention. The only subject before them was a request of the Sovereign, transmitted through the Lord-Lieutenant, that they would take into their consideration the most effectual means of consolidating into one lasting fabric the strength and power of the British Empire. There was no specific proposition at this time laid before the House. Taking advantage of the parliamentary etiquette of the day, which regarded the Speech from the Throne as that of the minister only, they were resolved to refuse this request. The fact was, they thought the Government was unprepared, and they wished to commit the country to a premature opinion on the question of a Union.

Lord Castlereagh was greatly disappointed with the result of the first debate. On the 21st of the month he had written to the Duke of Portland, " we reckon on from 160 to 170 with us, if they attend. Mr. Cooke thinks the Opposition can muster 100 certain, if they assemble."

The address was reported on the 24th of January. The tenth paragraph was as follows : " The unremitting activity with which our enemies persevere in their

founded, I am happy to say, has been disappointed by the event. I had been afraid that the interest of Ireland, on the abolition of her separate legislature, would come to be discussed in a hostile Parliament. But I can now state—and I wish when I speak that I could be heard by the whole of Ireland—that during the time that I have sat in the united Parliament I have found every question that related to the interests or security of that country entertained with indulgence, and treated with the most deliberate regard."—*Plunket's Life*, ii. 104.

avowed design of endeavouring to effect a separation of this kingdom from Great Britain must constantly engage our most earnest attention. And as your Majesty has condescended to express an anxious hope that this circumstance, joined to the sentiment of mutual affection and common interest, may dispose the Parliaments in both kingdoms to provide the most effectual means of maintaining and improving a connection essential to their common security, and of consolidating as far as possible into one firm and lasting fabric the strength, the power, and the resources of the British Empire, we shall not fail to give the fullest consideration to a communication of such momentous importance."

On this paragraph being read, Sir Lawrence Parsons opposed it on the ground that it pledged the House indirectly to the principle of a Union, and moved that it should be expunged. A long and animated discussion ensued, which lasted till six o'clock next morning, when a division took place. A hundred and nine voted for the omission of the paragraph and 104 for its retention, or, including tellers, 111 against 106 — a majority of five against the Government.

The principal speakers were: For the Government, Lord Castlereagh, the Attorney-General, Sir John Blaquiere, Mr. Corry, and Mr. (afterwards Sir) William Smith; against, Sir Lawrence Parsons, George Ponsonby, Mr. Dobbs,[1] Mr. Fitzgerald (late Prime Sergeant), and Mr. Tighe.

[1] This gentleman was a fanatic on prophecy, but on all other subjects he was an eloquent and sound-headed speaker and writer.

The Opposition had, during the debate, received an accession of four friends,[1] who had arrived in town in time to vote on the second occasion. General Taylor changed his mind during the discussion. Three members who had voted for the Government the first night were absent from illness.[2]

After this second debate was over George Ponsonby attempted to pledge the House against any change of opinion, and to preclude a future discussion of the question of Union. As the members assembled in the lobby were preparing to separate, Mr. Ponsonby requested them to return to the House for a short time, as he had business of the utmost importance for their consideration. When they had done so he, without further preface, moved "That this House will ever maintain the undoubted birthright of Irishmen by preserving an independent Parliament of Lords and Commons resident in this kingdom, as stated and approved by His Majesty and the British Parliament in 1782." This was moving as a substantive resolution the amendment which had been rejected the night before. Mr. Fortescue, an anti-Unionist, expressed his determination to oppose the resolution; Lord Cole, Mr. Acheson, Colonel Maxwell, J. C. Beresford, and Mr. French,[3] all

Lecky justly describes him as "of an eminently pure, gentle, honourable, and benevolent character."

[1] Hon. Wm. O'Callaghan, Henry Stewart, Francis Savage, John King.—*Corn. Corr.* iii. 49.

[2] Sir Hercules Langrishe, Mr. Conolly, Mr. John Beresford.—*Ib.*

[3] This gentleman is said to have refused an earldom offered to him if he would support a union. His son was created Lord De Freyne.—*Corn. Corr.* iii. 50.

strongly opposed to a Union, protested against it also. Mr. Ponsonby, seeing the House was against him, withdrew his motion.

This, early as it was in the struggle, was the turning point of the whole contest, and the impression made by the withdrawal of the motion was profound. Five of the six who protested against the resolution were county members, and J. C. Beresford (the sixth) was one of the members for the city of Dublin. It was evident that many of the Opposition, and particularly the country gentlemen among them, did not object to the principle of a Union, but merely objected to its being brought forward at that particular juncture. Their disinclination to adopt Ponsonby's motion was a tacit assent to the future discussion of the subject. Indeed the few words which Mr. Fortescue uttered, and in which the others concurred, leave no doubt on this point. "He did not wish to bind himself for ever. Possible circumstances might hereafter occur which might render that measure expedient for the Empire, and he did not approve of any determination which for ever closed the doors against any future discussion."[1] And we know that the Latouches, of whom there were four in this Parliament, and who all voted against the Government on this occasion, did so on the ground "that the time was not opportune."[2]

It was remarked that from the hour that this motion

[1] *Corn. Corr.* iii. 50. Barrington, *Rise and Fall, &c.*, 422.

[2] "John Latouche is decided in his opposition as to the time of bringing the measure forward, and says that all his family will vote on that idea."—Lord Camden to Lord Castlereagh, *Cast. Corr.* ii. 111.

H

was withdrawn the Union gained strength. From this onwards we shall find either an unwillingness on the part of the Opposition to risk a division, or a decided majority for the Government. Barrington tells us that when Ponsonby proposed to withdraw his motion, "chagrin and disappointment had changed sides, and the friends of the Union, who a moment before had considered their measure as nearly extinguished, rose upon their success, retorted in their turn and opposed its being withdrawn." Sir Henry Cavendish keenly and sarcastically remarked that it was a retreat after a victory.

It is worth our while at the end of these two debates to consider the position in which the House of Lords and the Commons stood. The Speech from the Throne had merely recommended to the consideration of Parliament the most effectual means of improving the connection with Great Britain, and of consolidating the power and resources of the British Empire. The Lords, by an overwhelming majority, had agreed to give "their fullest attention" to "considerations of such momentous importance." The Commons also on the 23rd of January undertook in nearly the same words to give their "fullest consideration to a communication of such momentous importance." But on the 24th they withdrew from this position, and expunged from their address the promise they had given the night before. Yet, at the same time, they refused, when Mr. Ponsonby's motion was made, to pledge themselves against a future consideration of the measure. This conduct of the Commons ought not to be attributed to inconstancy or capricious instability of opinion, but to the nature of the question. It was indeed a question of the most momentous kind, and on which any man might well entertain doubts. National dignity, the prestige and splendour of independence, and the fear of future neglect when incorporated with a more powerful kingdom, were on the one side. On the other, the prospect of allaying for ever internal dissensions, the assurance of security from external enemies, the hope of sharing the prosperity of Great Britain as an integral part of a mighty empire, and the consideration that emancipation might be granted to their fellow subjects without danger to the Constitution. It was no wonder that families were divided, though without rancour, on this great question. We find fathers and sons,[1] as well as brothers,[2] acting and voting on different sides. And, as the contest proceeded, many above all suspicion of their motives, were slowly converted, and espoused the side against which they had formerly acted and voted.[3]

During the second debate, Mr. William Smith delivered an extraordinarily able speech in favour of a Union, which made a great impression on the House, and afterwards when printed, on the country.[4] This, and

[1] As Lord Leitrim and his son Lord Clements; Lord Llandaff and his son Lord Mathew.
[2] The Duke of Leinster and his brother, Lord C. Fitzgerald; the brothers Skeffington, who represented the same town.
[3] As A. Ram, member for the county of Wexford, Dr. A. Browne, member for the University, Sir Hercules Langrishe, Richard Neville, Right Hon. David Latouche, Richard French, General Taylor, &c.
[4] This gentleman published three pamphlets on the Union. This speech was one; the other two were letters to Foster, the Speaker, and to Grattan. The study of these publications is absolutely indispensable to the comprehension of the question of union. The

Lord Clare's subsequent speech on the 10th of February, 1800, were the best argumentative speeches during the debates on the Union. Plunket's were too full of declamation, and not comparable to those he afterwards made in the Imperial Parliament on Catholic emancipation.

The only riot which took place in Ireland during the long discussion of the Union occurred on the evening when the Government was defeated. There was a general illumination in Dublin. The houses of the Unionists were attacked, and some Members of Parliament ill-treated. The military were called out, and several persons unfortunately lost their lives.

On the 28th of January Lord Castlereagh moved for an adjournment to the 7th of February, in order that the debates in the British Parliament should be made known and considered in Ireland. Sir John Parnell opposed the motion, but the Opposition did not venture on a division, and the House was adjourned to the day named.

The opponents of the Union were resolved to exert their utmost efforts to procure such a parliamentary pledge for the maintenance of the existing constitution as would oblige the Government finally to relinquish the scheme, though the House had declined to give such a pledge on the 24th of January. Accordingly Lord Corry on the 15th of February moved that the House should resolve itself into a general Committee on the

author was a member of a distinguished legal family. He was the son of Baron Smith, and was himself subsequently appointed a Baron of the Exchequer. He was father of the late T. B. C. Smith, Master of the Rolls.

state of the nation, and consider an address to the King, declaring a separate independent Parliament as essential to the interest and prosperity of Ireland. A division took place, when the numbers were 103 for the motion, against it 123, a majority of twenty for the Government.

This was the first decided success of the Government. The division was a great disappointment to the Opposition, who had hoped to carry the address. The tone of the debate was temperate, and some humorous speeches were delivered. The country gentlemen had quieted down. The most animated speaker was George Ponsonby, the representative of a family which had long exercised great influence.[1] Parsons, Parnell, and Plunket, did not speak. On the following day Lord Cornwallis wrote to the Duke of Portland: "The temper of the House was moderate; the country gentlemen all asserted their disposition to support Government, except upon the measure of Union; and in general they wished it to be understood that the address was by no means designed to pledge the House irrevocably against a Union, if the circumstances of the kingdom should materially alter."[2]

One of the strongest arguments for a Union was derived from the possibility that two independent legislatures might take different views on any international question. Pitt had relied on this possibility in his speech in the British Parliament, recommending an incorporation of the two legislatures. The Unionists urged this reason, and pointed, as an illustration, to the

[1] *Corn. Corr.* iii. 324.   [2] *Ib.* iii. 64.

conduct of the Irish Parliament on the Regency question. To deprive their opponents of this argument, the anti-Unionists brought forward a Regency Bill, which provided that in all cases, the regal powers of the Empire should be administered by the same person in Ireland as exercised such powers in Great Britain, and that the person exercising these powers should be subject to the same restrictions and limitations in both kingdoms. This was indeed eating the leek. The Opposition were willing to make what was really a legislative apology for the action which the Irish Parliament had taken in 1789. When the Bill was committed Lord Castlereagh pointed out its inadequacy, that it only provided for one of the cases in which a difference of opinion might arise, and that it was necessary to dry up for ever the source of such international disagreements, that the cases of war, treaties with foreign powers, and other matters, might lead to variance of decision, and that these emergencies were not provided for in any way by the Bill.

On the 11th of April, the House resolved itself into a Committee in order to consider this Bill. The Speaker, Mr. Foster, took advantage of this circumstance to deliver his sentiments against a Union in a speech of four hours.[1] A debate followed, in which that measure was the principal topic. Little was said about the Bill which was before the Committee. When the Bill was discussed again on the 18th of April, the majority did not think it provided an adequate remedy for the evils of parlia-

[1] In this debate Mr. Foster described Pitt's speech, recommending a union, in the British Parliament, as a "paltry production."

mentary variance which it was intended to remove. It was postponed to the 1st of August, and then dropped.

The proposal of the Regency Bill was of great service to the cause of the Union. The Bill was brought forward to diminish the necessity of a Union by removing the possibility of any difference between the Parliaments of the two kingdoms. By bringing it forward the anti-Unionists admitted the dangers of the connection as it then stood; by dropping it they confessed their inability to remove those dangers, unless they adopted a Union and renounced the settlement of 1782.

A debate took place on the 15th of May. A question was asked respecting the refusal of the Escheatorship of Munster, the equivalent in Ireland of the Chiltern Hundreds, to Colonel Cole. The subject of the Union was dragged into the discussion, and some violent speeches were made. Plunket, George Ponsonby, Mr. Dobbs and others took part in the debate. The motion for an adjournment to the 1st of June was carried in a thin House by Government, the voting being forty-seven to thirty-two. This was the last discussion on the Union during this year, the House being subsequently prorogued to the 15th of January, 1800.

At this time Grattan was not in Parliament. He took his seat, as one of the members for Wicklow, on the night of the 15th of January following, or rather on the morning of the 16th.

Less than four months had elapsed since the opening of Parliament, and it is evident that the opponents of a Union had lost ground. There was a steady phalanx against them in the Lords that had spoken with no uncertain voice on the subject. The Government were unprepared when the anti-Unionists prematurely sprung the discussion on them in the Commons, for no specific proposal had been made, and the Speech from the Throne had merely invited them to consider the most effectual means of uniting more closely the two kingdoms. The opponents of the Union were beaten in the first contest. They succeeded in the second. But this was a Pyrrhic victory, for on the same night the most considerable portion of their party refused to pledge themselves against the future consideration of the measure. On the 28th of January they did not venture to try their strength on Lord Castlereagh's motion for an adjournment. On the 15th of February they united all their forces to carry Lord Corry's motion for a general Committee on the state of the nation, and an address declaring that a separate Parliament was essential to the prosperity of Ireland, and they were defeated by the decided majority of twenty. On the 11th of April the proposal of a Regency Bill told heavily against them, inasmuch as it admitted the flaw in the connection between the two countries; the dropping of it confessed the inability of the anti-Unionists to cure that flaw without a Union.

The fact was that the opponents of the Union were a composite and discordant party, united only in their opposition to that measure. Many of them, particularly their leaders—as Mr. Foster, Sir John Parnell, the Right Honourable George Ogle, the Duke of Leinster, Lords Charlemont, Farnham, and Enniskillen—were opposed to the full emancipation of the Catholics and their admission to Parliament. The Government was at one time afraid that the Opposition would tempt the Catholics to array themselves against the Union by a motion in favour of emancipation,[1] and such an inducement was offered to that body by some of the anti-Unionists who were least indisposed against them.[2] The Union could not have been carried against the wishes of the Catholics. The anti-Unionists knew this well, and yet they never ventured, as a body, to bring forward the question of emancipation, for they were well aware that such a proposal would have split their party in two. Nor were they ever able, during the long contest of the Union, to induce the Catholics to join them in their opposition to that measure. The Catholics sympathised much more strongly with the English Government than with the Irish Parliament,[3] and distrusted an assembly which was filled with their enemies. As their leaders —the Catholic Archbishop of Dublin, and Lords Fingall and Kenmare—told Lord Cornwallis, they did not think the Irish Parliament capable of entering into a cool and dispassionate consideration of their claims, and put all their trust in the hoped-for united Parliament.[4] The principal men among them believed that it was under the pressure of the anti-Catholic party that the English Cabinet had yielded upon the question of Lord Fitzwilliam's recall. "This consideration," says Mr. Plunket, "will help to explain

[1] *Corn. Corr.* iii. 53.
[2] *Ib.* iii. 52.
[3] Lecky, iv. 462.
[4] *Corn. Corr.* iii. 8.

the case with which Lord Cornwallis prevailed with the Roman Catholic Episcopacy to lend him their assistance in carrying the Union, without any distinct assurance on his part that the terms which they demanded would be conceded."[2]

[1] *Life of Lord Plunket*, i. 279.

CHAPTER V.

Sentiments of the Protestant community on a Union.—The measure at first disapproved of.—Change of opinion in its favour.—Declarations and petitions for and against it.—Bribery by the Opposition.—Attempts of the anti-Unionists to excite the country against the Union.

For upwards of eighty years the maligners of the Irish Union have adopted one system of calumny —for line of argument it cannot be called. They take a fact here and a fact there; an extract from a letter here and another there; they then carefully piece them together. If the patchwork be deemed insufficient, they fill up the pattern with unscrupulous declamation and glaring misrepresentation. Aware that, at first and before its terms were made known, the Union was unpopular with the majority of Protestants, the aristocratic proprietors of boroughs, and the members of the smaller corporations — of which there were more than eighty—they represent the Union as having been passed against the will of the nation. These critics carefully avoid the development of events and the chronological order of occurrences. They mix up what ought to be kept separate, and laboriously conceal the fact that during the long discussion of the measure, the country was converted in its favour—a conversion so striking and remarkable that even the Opposition were obliged to admit it, for in the debates of 1800 one of the violent members of the anti-Unionist party complained in the House of Commons "that the people had deserted them."[1]

The principal opponents of the Irish Union were— the inhabitants of Dublin, who feared that their city would be reduced from a capital to a provincial town; the borough proprietors and their numerous dependants; the official classes, who were wedded to the existing system of things; the lawyers, who dreaded the removal of the law courts to London; and the corporations of the smaller boroughs, who foresaw their own dissolution, and the loss of their influence. Of these opponents, the barristers were the noisiest. They had always considered a seat in the legislature as the road to preferment, and there were fifty of them in the last Parliament of Ireland.[2]

The Orangemen declined to act as a body in the discussion of the Union. Their Grand Master, Thomas Verner, generally known as the Prince of Orange, advised them, while exercising their individual rights as Members of Parliament, grand jurors, freeholders or burgesses, to abstain from taking any part as a distinct society. After a few mutinies in some lodges, the Orangemen acquiesced in this decision, and remained neutral as a body during the contest.[3]

[1] *Corn. Corr.* iii. 249.   [2] *Ib.* 81.
[3] On one occasion thirty-two lodges disapproved of Mr. Verner's advice, but the good sense of the Society prevailed.—*Belf. News Letter*, March 4th, 1800.

We have already seen that the first proposal of a Union was unfavourably received by the majority of the Protestants. Before the 1st of February, 1799, and therefore before its terms and conditions had become known throughout Ireland, the counties of Louth, Tyrone, Cavan, Clare, Tipperary, and Dublin, the cities of Dublin and Galway, and the University of Dublin, held meetings and came to resolutions adverse to a Union. But as the terms leaked out, and it transpired that the interests of the different bodies likely to be affected by the Union would be tenderly dealt with, the opinion of the public veered round steadily in its favour. As the opposition to the measure diminished throughout the country, the majority in Parliament in its favour regularly increased. Our readers will remember that it was on Lord Corry's motion to take into consideration the state of the nation on the 15th of February, 1799, that the Government obtained their first decided success of a majority of twenty. Nor was it long until signs of a change of opinion manifested themselves out of Parliament. As early as March 28th, 1799, Lord Cornwallis, who had been greatly discouraged by the division of the 24th of January, writes : " The opinion of the loyal part of the public is, from everything that I can learn, changing fast in favour of the Union."[1] And the editor of his correspondence tells us that "this change of feeling in regard to the Union was caused principally by its having transpired that material alterations would be made in the details of the measure." On the following day Lord Cornwallis wrote again, " Much good effect has resulted

[1] *Corn. Corr.* iii. 81.

from the discussion in England, and I have reason to believe that a change of sentiment is gradually diffusing itself."[1] On the last day of the same month Colonel Littlehales informs Lord Donoughmore, who had written to him respecting the change of opinion which his lordship had observed in his part of the country—Tipperary, " The alteration in the minds of many is obvious in other parts of the kingdom, and is a confirmation of its wisdom and justice. It is by reflection only that its value can be really estimated."[2] In April, Lord Castlereagh tells the Duke of Portland, " I can confidently assure your Grace that the measure of Union is making its way in proportion as it is canvassed and understood."[3] On the 5th of June Lord Altamont writes from Sligo, "I have found to my infinite surprise that the county and town of Sligo, without the slightest interference, and against all their representatives, are decided friends of the Union. I know of no part of Ireland where the *unbiassed* mind of the public is so generally with it. Roscommon is against it; but for that, the bulk, or indeed, the entire of the province, might be considered as pledged to the measure, or ready to be so."[4] We shall shortly see that a few months later the county of Roscommon also declared for the Union, so that when Parliament met in the following January the province of Connaught was pledged to that measure. On the 22nd of June Lord Cornwallis informs the Duke of Portland, " Within the last month I think I am justified in stating to your Grace that we have sensibly gained strength."

[1] *Corn. Corr.* iii. 83.   [2] *Ib.* 84.
[3] *Cast. Corr.* ii. 274.   [4] *Ib.* ii. 327.

In this letter he also tells the Duke that "Galway, King's County, Mayo, and Kerry, have already come forward; Cork, Mayo, and Kerry, with a unanimity unexampled on any public measure. The temper of Dublin remains strongly adverse, but not in the degree it did. Some of the commercial body have altered their sentiments."[1] In August he writes again to the Duke, "The accession of Tipperary to those counties before declared gives us the entire province of Munster; and its weight will be the more authoritative, as it is an inland county, and not decided merely by commercial prospects."[2]

In the same month Mr. Dawson writes from the county of Down, "I find men from the counties of Cavan and Monaghan here, with whom I talked much in the beginning of July in their own counties, and found them much against the measure. I have great satisfaction in being able to tell you that they are much brought about, and that I consider them as gained."[3] In September, Dr. Moylan, Catholic Bishop of Cork, writes from Dublin to Sir J. C. Hippesley, "I am happy to tell you it (the Union) is working its way and daily gaining ground on the public opinion. Several counties which appeared most averse to it have now declared for it, and I have no doubt but with the blessing of God it will be effected, notwithstanding the violent opposition of Mr. Foster and his party, who will strain every nerve and move heaven and earth to prevent its succeeding. In this city, where the outcry against it has been so

---

[1] *Cast. Corr.* ii. 336. [2] *Ib.* ii. 372.
[3] Mr. Dawson to Mr. Marshall, *Cast. Corr.* ii. 374.

very violent, it is becoming every day less unpopular."[1]
In the same month Mr. Marsden writes to Lord Castlereagh, then absent in London, "I have everything encouraging to pronounce on the progress which union makes. It is going on silently and persuasively, and it is by no means desirable that this progression should be disturbed for some time to come."[2] On the 9th of September Lord Waterford writes: "I do not hesitate in pronouncing that the opinion of the county and city of Waterford is nearly unanimous in favour of union."[3] On the 22nd Lord Cornwallis writes to his friend, General Ross: "We were of opinion that the immediate meeting of Parliament might put to some hazard the success of our great measure of Union which is now daily gaining ground as well in, as out of Parliament."[4] On the 12th of October, the Catholic Archbishop of Dublin writes to Mr. Marshall: "You will observe by our public papers that the question of Union is daily gaining ground."[5] In November, Lord Cornwallis informs his friend again: "The Union is, I trust, making progress. The great body of the people in general, and of the Catholics in particular, are decidedly for it, and from what I hear of the liberal disposition of the British Government, I think if we can once bring the Parliament of Ireland to enter into a discussion of the terms, it cannot fail of success."[6] In January, 1800, Mr. Bradshaw writes from Belfast: "Until very lately Union was a subject very little talked about, less understood.

[1] *Cast. Corr.* ii. 399.
[2] *Ib.* ii. 406.
[3] *Ib.* ii. 394.
[4] *Corn. Corr.* iii. 133.
[5] *Cast. Corr.* ii. 418.
[6] *Corn. Corr.* iii. 143.

It has now become a very general topic, and although the great majority approve of it, we have some dissentients. It is pretty nearly a general wish that this great object may be speedily settled, as the most certain means of for ever quieting the unhappy distractions that have too long tormented this country, as well as procuring for us benefits highly essential both to our commerce and constitution."[1]

Lord Cornwallis had long been of opinion that the opponents of the Union were chiefly those who had an immediate and private interest in the maintenance of the local Parliament, and that the opposition to that measure proceeded for the most part from the borough proprietors and the persons throughout the country whose influence depended on the existence of the smaller corporations. He resolved to learn for himself the sentiments of the people on the subject.[2] He therefore determined to pay visits to the south and north, and observe the disposition of the country. Accordingly in July and August, 1799, he made a short tour through the counties of Kilkenny, Cork, Waterford, and Tipperary. The result proved the accuracy of his judgment, and the cities and towns through which he passed vied with each other in presenting addresses in favour of the Union.

[1] *Cast. Corr.* iii. 224.
[2] "This tour will enable me to speak with more precision of the state of the public mind on the Union than I have hitherto been able to do. My observations have as yet been altogether confined to Dublin, which is certainly the point of resistance."—*Cast. Corr.* ii. 352.

In Kilkenny he received two addresses "expressive of the most earnest desire for a union :"[1]

> From the Catholic inhabitants of the city.
> From the Corporation.

In Cork he received seven addresses in favour of the measure :

> From the Catholic inhabitants of the city.[2]
> From the High Sheriff and Grand Jury of the county.[3]
> From the High Sheriffs and Grand Jury of the city.[4]
> From the Protestant Bishop and Clergy of the dioceses of Cork and Ross.[5]
> From the Mayor, Sheriffs, and Common Council of the city.[6]
> From the Provost, Burgesses, and Freemen of Bandon.[7]
> From the Mayor, Burgesses, and Commonalty of Youghal[8]

In Limerick he received two addresses:

> One from the Merchants and Traders of the city.[9]
> One from the Protestant Bishop and Clergy of the city.[10]

---

[1] *Corn. Corr.* iii. 119.
[2] Advert. *Belfast News Letter*, 23rd August.   [3] *Ib.* 27th Aug.
[4] *Ib.*   [5] *Ib.*   [6] *Ib.*   [7] *Ib.* Sep. 3rd.
[8] *Ib.*   [9] *Ib.* 23rd Aug.   [10] *Ib.*

OF GREAT BRITAIN AND IRELAND. 115

In Waterford he received three addresses :

> One from the Noblemen, Clergy, Gentry, and inhabitants of the county.[1]
> One from the Mayor, Sheriffs, and citizens of the city.[2]
> One from the Protestant Clergy resident in the city.[3]

In Tipperary he received two addresses :

> One from the Catholic inhabitants of Tipperary and Cahir.[4]
> One from the Freemen and inhabitants of Clonmel, the county town and its neighbourhood.[5]

At the same time the nobility, gentry, clergy, and freeholders of this county drew up another address to His Majesty in favour of the Union.[6]

During this southern tour, or shortly afterwards, Lord Cornwallis also received similar addresses from :

> The Catholic inhabitants of Wexford and its vicinity.[7]
> The Catholic inhabitants of New Ross and its neighbourhood.[8]
> The Catholics of the county Longford.[9]
> The Catholic Clergy of the diocese of Elphin and county of Roscommon.[10]
> The inhabitants of Sligo.[11]
> The inhabitants of Kinsale.[12]

[1] Advert. *Belfast News Letter*, 27th Aug.   [2] *Ib.*   [3] *Ib.*
[4] *Ib.* 3rd Sept.   [5] *Ib.*   [6] *Ib.* 10th Sep.   [7] *Ib.* 19th Nov.
[8] *Ib.* 15th Nov.   [9] *Ib.* 1st Oct.   [10] *Ib.* 10th Jan. 1800.
[11] *Ib.* 31st Jan.   [12] *Ib.* 29th Nov.

Lord Cornwallis was well satisfied with the results of his southern journey, and thus expresses his feelings: "I returned to town on Friday from my southern tour, and am happy to have it in my power to convey to your Grace the most satisfactory accounts of that part of the kingdom, as well in point of tranquillity as in general good disposition towards the Government and cordial approbation of the measure of Union. This sentiment is confined to no particular class or description of men; but equally pervades both the Catholic and Protestant bodies, and I was much gratified in observing that those feelings which originated with the higher orders have, in a great degree, extended themselves to the body of the people. Were the Commons of Ireland as naturally connected with the people as they are in England, and as liable to receive their impressions, with the prospects we have out of doors I should feel that the question was, in a great degree, carried. But your Grace is so well acquainted with the constitution of the assembly in which this question is to be prosecuted, and must be aware how anxiously personal objects will be connected with this measure, which goes to new-model the public consequence of every man in Parliament, and to diminish the authority of the most powerful, that your Grace will feel, however advantageous it is for the Government to carry the public sentiment with it, that distinct interests are there to be encountered which will require all the exertions and all the means of Government to overcome, and which may still very much delay and impede the accomplishment of this great settlement."[1]

[1] *Corn. Corr.* iii. 121.

In the early part of October, Lord Cornwallis proceeded to the north, where his experience was equally satisfactory. During his northern journey he received addresses in favour of the Union from the following towns and public bodies:—

    From the Catholic inhabitants of Dundalk.[1]
    From the Corporation of the same town.[2]
    From the Corporation of Belfast.[3]
    From the electors and principal inhabitants of Antrim.[4]
    From the Sovereign and Corporation of Armagh.[5]
    From the Protestant Bishop and Clergy of the diocese of Dromore.[6]
    From the Corporation of Coleraine.[7]
    From the Noblemen, Clergy, and freeholders of the county of Londonderry. [8]
    From the Mayor, Community and citizens of the city of Londonderry.[9]
    From the Corporation and principal inhabitants of Newtownlimavady.[10]
    From the Warden and inhabitants of Lifford.[11]
    From the Merchants and inhabitants of the town and neighbourhood of Castlefinn.[12]
    From the Provost, Corporation and inhabitants of Strabane.[13]
    From the Provost, Grand Jury and Corporation of Monaghan.[14]

[1] *Belfast News Letter*, 15th Oct.   [2] *Ib.*
[3] *Ib.* 11th Oct.   [4] *Ib.*   [5] *Ib.* 15th Oct.   [6] *Ib.*
[7] *Ib.* 29th Oct.   [8] *Ib.* 25th Oct.   [9] *Ib.*   [10] *Ib.*
[11] *Ib.* 29th Oct.   [12] *Ib.*   [13] *Ib.* 1st Nov.   [14] *Ib.* 15th Nov.

Lord Cornwallis gives us his opinion of the manner in which he was received in the north. "My northern tour has answered my most sanguine expectations. At Dundalk, the first place that I visited, exclusive of the address from the Corporation, which is under the influence of Lord Roden, I received an unasked and unsought for address from the Roman Catholic inhabitants in favour of the Union. I did not enter the county of Down, lest that proud leviathan, Lord Downshire, should call it a declaration of war, but I was received with open arms at Belfast, and throughout the counties of Antrim and Derry the cry for a union is almost unanimous."[1]

At the same time, he writes to the Duke of Portland. "At Antrim, Coleraine, Newtownlimavady, and all the places through which I passed, addresses were presented, and the words 'principal inhabitants' were always inserted as well as 'the Corporation.' At Londonderry, my reception was cordial and flattering beyond expression; the county as well as the city addressed; the town was illuminated, and 'success to the Union' resounded from every quarter."[2]

The cases of the towns of Wexford and Galway are remarkable, and illustrate the change of opinion which had come over the country. Richard Nevill had represented Wexford for twenty-eight years. In January, 1799, he had voted against the consideration of the Union. The town, we are told, "was completely under the influence of Richard Nevill and a few

---

[1] *Corn. Corr.* iii. 140.   [2] *Ib.*

others."[1] Yet, in January, 1800, a meeting of the freeholders, who amounted to between 800 and 900,[2] was held in favour of the Union, and this gentleman was unanimously requested to use "his utmost exertions to have it carried into immediate execution on terms impartial, liberal and honourable." Mr. Nevill took the hint, and voted for the measure in 1800.[3]

The city of Galway affords even a more striking example of this change of opinion. In January, 1799, the town had declared explicitly against a union. Plowden tells us, "the resolutions of a meeting at Galway were particularly strong; reprobating the attempts of the Unionists as unconstitutional and arbitrary; denying the power of the representatives of the people to vote away the independence of the realm, condemning the transfer of the right of legislation to any foreign country without the general consent of the people as equivalent to the dissolution of the existing government, and as a procedure which from its tendency to anarchy ought to be resisted; and stigmatising as enemies to their country all the supporters of such a measure."[4]

Galway had a large constituency, the voters amounting to between 1,500 and 2,000.[5] On the 2nd of

[1] *Report on the Representation*, presented to the Volunteer Convention, Dublin, 1784.   [2] *Ib.*
[3] See the Address, *Belfast News Letter*, 17th Jan. 1800.
[4] *Review of the State of Ireland*, vol. ii., pt. ii., 824.
[5] In 1784, before the admission of the Catholics to the franchise, the voters numbered between 500 and 600. In 1829 no change in the law having been made since 1793, they numbered 2,300.— See Lynch's *Law of Elections in Ireland*.

August, 1799, a meeting of the electors and inhabitants was held, at which the town retracted its former opinion. The following resolution was at this meeting unanimously passed, "That an incorporative union of the legislatures of the two countries (though that measure, when it was first presented to our view, and before the terms upon which it was proposed to be effected were disclosed, impressed itself rather unfavourably upon some of our minds) is, in our opinion, upon mature and deliberative consideration, the system of relation which of every other is the best fitted to secure to both countries all the blessings of connection, and to protect them against all the evils of separation."[1]

Nor were the counties behind the towns in manifesting this change of opinion. In June, 1799, Cork, Kerry, Mayo, King's County, and Galway declared for the Union, "Cork, Mayo, and Kerry with unanimity unexampled on any public measure."[2] Galway county in a "meeting the fullest ever known,"[3] declared for the Union, and instructed its members to vote for that measure. In August, the counties of Tipperary, Waterford and Wexford; in September, Londonderry, Limerick and Antrim; in November, Tyrone and Clare; in December, Donegal; in January, 1800, Armagh, Roscommon and Kilkenny; in February, Downshire, Monaghan, Leitrim and Meath; in March,

---

[1] *Belfast News Letter*, 6th Sep. 1799.
[2] Lord Cornwallis to Duke of Portland.—*Cast. Corr.* ii. 336.
[3] "We have succeeded at a county meeting of Galway, the fullest ever known, and have carried an address and instructions to the ministers."—*Corn. Corr.* iii. 129.

Westmeath. The Catholic freeholders and inhabitants of the counties of Kilkenny, Longford, Leitrim and Roscommon, separately addressed or declared for the Union. But a more particular consideration of the support which the Catholics gave to the Union is reserved for the next chapter.[1]

On the 5th of February, 1800, and before some of the counties had declared for the measure, Lord Castlereagh summed up in the House of Commons the amount of support which the Union had received throughout the country. "The great body of the landed property of Ireland was friendly to the principle, and the two houses of Parliament particularly; three-fourths of the landed property were amongst its supporters; nineteen counties, five-sevenths of Ireland in superficial extent had come forward in its support. He did not say that these counties were unanimous in approving the measure; complete unanimity was not to be hoped upon any great political question; but he would say a very great majority of those counties favoured the measure. All the great commercial towns, save Dublin and Drogheda, had declared in favour of it."[2] In a subsequent debate, he stated that seventy-four declarations had been made in favour of a Union by public bodies; that nineteen of them proceeded from the freeholders of counties, and many of the remainder from the chief towns and corporations.[3] We have seen that this was an underestimate, that twenty-two counties had declared for the

---

[1] The declarations of the counties are to be found as advertisements in the *Belfast News Letter*, in the different months.
[2] *Parl. Deb.*, Moore, Dublin, 1800.   [3] *Corn. Corr.* iii. 203.

Union, and if we add to these the declarations of the Catholic freeholders of the counties of Kilkenny, Longford, Leitrim, and Roscommon, we find twenty-six declarations from the freeholders of counties. Subsequently, on the 2nd of April, Lord Castlereagh in a letter to the Under-Secretary of State, sent "an abstract of the best analysis we have been able to make of the annual landed income of the supporters and opposers of union in the two Houses of Parliament. I believe the whole is under estimated."[1]

	For.	Against.
Resident Peers	£606,800	£179,000
Bishops	80,000	6,000
Commoners	268,900	144,500
	955,700	329,500
Absentee Peers	102,500	29,000
	£1,058,200	£358,500

On the 4th of March, 1800, George Ponsonby stated in the House that the people of Ireland were opposed to the Union, and that the anti-Union petitions on the table proved this. He went on to say that petitions against that measure had been received from twenty-six counties and several great towns, and also from the corporation and guilds of the metropolis. Petitions to Parliament are often spontaneous, and really express the wishes of the people. They also may be, and often are, concocted or worked up by able and efficient wire-pullers. It is worth our while to examine these petitions

[1] *Corn. Corr.* iii 224.

on which Mr. Ponsonby relied, and to see to what class they belong. They are still to be read in the journals of the Commons.

There are fifty-four petitions in these journals for the year 1800, which are entitled, "Against a Union," and only two in its favour. There are none for 1799, and none were presented to the House of Lords. The anti-Unionists avoided the Upper House, where there was a strong majority against them, and naturally preferred to direct their petitions to the Commons, where their recognised leader was Speaker, and where they had a strong and compact body in their favour. The Unionists just as naturally avoided the Commons, and preferred to make their sentiments known in county declarations, or in addresses to the Lord-Lieutenant or the King.

When we come to examine these fifty-four petitions, we find that five of them are not petitions against the Union at all, but merely prayers for compensation " in the event of a union." Three are from individuals or commercial firms, and may be dismissed as not being representative of the public voice. We shall consider the forty-six which remain. Of these, eight come from Dublin alone : one from the City Corporation, and seven from guilds, as booksellers, carpenters, bricklayers, &c. Thirty-eight proceed from twenty-five counties and eleven towns, Kilkenny and Drogheda sending in two each.[1]

All these forty-six petitions arrived as it were in a batch. They were presented between the 4th of February, 1800, and the 14th of the following month. The

[1] Not 26 counties, as Mr. Ponsonby stated.

Parliament of 1799 had risen, and the Lord-Lieutenant had made his parting speech on the 1st of June in that year. Seven months elapse, during which we hear of no petitions or addresses to the King or the Viceroy against a Union. It is true that the Sovereign had recommended the measure to the consideration of the Irish Parliament, but this was no reason why His Majesty should be left in ignorance of what, the Opposition alleged, was the real sense of the country. One would have thought that petitioning and addressing was the best means known to our constitution of enlightening the Sovereign as to the real wishes of his subjects. The reason of the sudden activity of the anti-Unionists in presenting these petitions is not far to seek. They were alarmed by the declarations and addresses which were made and published during the interval which elapsed between June 1799, and the opening of Parliament in 1800. They therefore collected all their forces to make a last effort against the Union. The time of presenting these petitions and a certain similarity of expression which runs through them all, may be accounted for by the following circular or letter missive which, with its inclosure, was sent round to every part of Ireland.

"DUBLIN, *Jan.* 20, 1800.

"SIR,

"A number of gentlemen of both Houses of Parliament, of whom thirty-eight represent counties, have authorised us to acquaint you that it is their opinion that petitions to Parliament, declaring the real sense of the freeholders of the kingdom on the subject of a Legislative Union, would at this time be highly expedient; and if such a proceeding shall have your approbation, we are to request you will use your influence to have such a petition from your county without delay.

"We have the honour to be, Sir,
"Your most obedient, humble servants,
"DOWNSHIRE,
"CHARLEMONT,[1]
"W. B. PONSONBY."

The inclosure was a form of petition which was to represent the "real sense" of the country. "To the Knights, Citizens, and Burgesses in Parliament assembled. The humble petition of the undersigned freeholders of the County —— showeth that at this awful and alarming crisis we feel ourselves called upon to declare our opinion that a Legislative Union with Great Britain to be[2] a dangerous innovation, fraught with ruin to the constitutional independence, commercial interests, and general prosperity of the kingdom. That this measure, by depriving us of a resident and protective legislature, under which our country has hitherto prospered beyond example, by increasing the number of absentees and the consequent drain of our wealth, must augment the discontents of the kingdom, and thereby endanger the connection between Great Britain and Ireland, which we are determined to support with our lives and fortunes. That we rely, therefore, with unshaken confidence on the wisdom and justice of this honourable House, that it will maintain to us and our posterity

[1] Volunteer Charlemont died 4th of August, 1799. This was his son.
[2] *Sic*, as given in Lord Clare's speech.

unimpaired, that sacred constitution which is our birthright, which has been the source of every blessing to the island, and the enjoyment of which we deem inseparable from our existence as a free people."

We have the answers to this circular appeal in the forty-six petitions to the House of Commons. Those from the freeholders of the towns were all presented between the 4th and 15th of February, the latest being on the 14th. Those from the counties were laid on the table between the 4th and the 24th of the same month, except that from the Queen's County, which was presented on the 1st of March. The other petitions from the Corporation of Dublin and the Guilds were presented between the 4th of February and the 14th of March.

This was an instance, on an extensive scale, of what Lord Coke calls "auricular confession," where you present your own opinion to another, and, at the same time, press him to further and recommend it. The scheme of circulating a ready-made petition in order to collect the unbiassed sentiments of the people, was no doubt a proceeding calculated to relieve the class which was addressed from all difficulty of deliberation. But what weight can we attach to petitions so sought for and so obtained? When we remember that the Administration was contending with a powerful local oligarchy, which had so long held the government of Ireland in its hands, and which was supported by hangers-on in every county and by all the petty corporations in the country, we can only wonder that instead of forty-six petitions, there were not many times that number. Nothing proves so clearly as the feeble response made to the circular letter, that the people were satisfied with the project of Union, and that they had deserted the Opposition. If we keep in mind the dates of the circular and of the presentation of the petitions, it will appear that there was not a single spontaneous petition against the Union from any public body throughout the whole of Ireland.

The two noblemen who had signed the circular were present in the House of Lords when it was referred to by Lord Clare, in his great speech of the 10th of February, 1800. "But the active exertions of itinerant lords and commoners were not deemed sufficient for the occasion, and we have seen a consular authority assumed by two noble lords and a right hon. commoner, who have issued their letter-missive to every part of the kingdom, commanding the people, in the name of a number of gentlemen of both Houses of Parliament, to come forward with petitions condemning in terms of violence and indignation the measure of Union, prior to its discussion in Parliament. . . . . Let me ask the two noble lords who have thus put themselves forward, what are the exclusive pretensions of them and their right hon. colleague to guide the public opinion ? Let me ask them by what authority they have issued their letter-missive to every corner of the kingdom, commanding the people to subscribe an instrument fraught with foul and violent misrepresentation ? And let me ask them, is there salvation for this country under the present Government and constitution, when men of their rank and situation can stoop to so shabby and wicked an artifice to excite popular outcry against the declared sense of both Houses of Parliament?"

There can be no doubt also that the anti-Unionists had recourse to a system of open and general bribery. Of this we have both direct and circumstantial evidence. On the 29th of January, 1800, Lord Castlereagh writes to the Duke of Portland: "It is said that a very considerable sum has been subscribed for the purpose of buying seats to resist the Union. If I can believe a Member of Parliament who has now a seat vacant, 4000*l*. was offered him for the return in Mr. Curran's favour. Two lawyers .... have been returned for two seats which we had reason to count on."[1] On the 7th of February, he states to the same Minister that Mr. Whaley was "absolutely bought by the Opposition stock purse. He received, I understand, 2000*l*. down, and is to receive as much more after the service is performed. We have undoubted proofs, though not such as we can disclose, that they are enabled to offer as high as 5000*l*. for an individual vote."[2] On the following day Lord Cornwallis writes to his brother, "One (of our supporters) was bought during the debate, Jerusalem Whaley, the Chancellor's brother-in-law. The enemy, to my certain knowledge, offer 5000*l*. ready money for a vote.[3] The editor, through whose hands all Lord Cornwallis' papers and correspondence passed,

---

[1] *Corn. Corr.* iii. 174.   [2] *Ib.* 182.
[3] *Ib.* iii. 184. Mr. Whaley got the name of "Jerusalem" from a bet, said to have been for 20,000*l*., that he would walk, except where a sea-passage was unavoidable, to Jerusalem and back within twelve months.

declares it is certain that large sums were spent in bribery by the Opposition. Barrington practically admits this.[1] Lord Charlemont, when he was accused in the Upper House by Lord Clare of subscribing to a stock-purse collected for this purpose, proved "pretty distinctly by his defence to the charge, that a Consular Exchequer did exist for the corruption of Parliament."[2] And Grattan's son informs us in the life of his father: "One of the plans adopted and acted on by the Opposition, was to bring into Parliament members to vote against the Union; it amounted, in fact, to a project to out-buy the minister. . . . To carry into effect this measure a subscription was opened, the names set down were numerous, and the sums considerable; in a short time 100,000*l.* was subscribed."[3] The author then goes on to tell us the same story of Mr. Whaley, how this gentleman, who had voted for the Union in 1799, received 4000*l.* for voting against it in 1800.

The Opposition boasted that they had a stock-purse, and that they had collected a sum of 100,000*l.*[4] Subscriptions were openly solicited in the streets of Dublin to a fund for defeating the measure of Union.[5] On one occasion, in February, 1800, twelve of their supporters, of whom Mr. Whaley was one, left the Government.[6] How are we to account for this whole-

[1] *Rise and Fall, &c.*, 460, note 488.
[2] *Corn. Corr.* iii. 186.   [3] *Grattan's Life*, v. 71.
[4] *Corn. Corr.* iii. 174.
[5] "I know that subscriptions are openly solicited in the streets of the metropolis to a fund for defeating the measure of Union."—Lord Clare in House of Lords, 10th Feb. 1800.
[6] *Corn. Corr.* iii. 183.

sale desertion? Members of Parliament are generally men of a mature time of life, and change of opinion is not instantaneous in a middle-aged bosom. The country was at this time disposed in favour of the Union. Making every allowance for pressure from a few of the constituencies, it is impossible to believe that these sudden conversions were the results of reflection, or arose from other than interested motives.

When men like Plunket, Foster, and Bushe, made use of such childish arguments, as that the Irish legislature was not competent to enact a Union, and that the settlement of 1782 precluded an international treaty between two independent kingdoms—when the leaders of the Opposition spoke sedition, and by prophesying future treason, encouraged it [1]— and when the rank and file of the same party talked of shedding their blood in defence of their local Parliament, and urged that the only reason Pitt had in recommending a Union was to get possession of the Irish purse—we may be certain that its supporters felt the weakness of a cause which was sustained by such logic. If, however, the anti-Unionists were inferior in argument and reasoning, they could at least attempt to harass the Government by alarming the country and exciting its prejudices against the Union. For this purpose they had recourse to every means in their power. In the north the farmers were told that the Union was a project of Mr. Pitt to lay a tax of five shillings on every wheel, and two shillings on every loom, that when the Parliament was taken away

[1] *Corn. Corr.* iii. 240-1, 213.

all their leases would be broken, and the land relet at higher rents, and that this was the reason that so many of the landlords were in favour of the measure.¹ In the south, where the mass of the people were Catholics, different tactics were employed. Dr. Moylan, Catholic Bishop of Cork, informs us that "it was industriously propagated, no doubt by the enemies of the Union, that this measure, once effected, would preclude for ever the Roman Catholics of the kingdom from the hopes of further emancipation, and that under the Imperial Parliament the junto who oppressed them would still prevail and hold the reins of the Government of the country."² And on the 10th of February, 1800, Lord Clare in the House of Lords enumerated some of the means to which the anti-Unionists had resorted. "To their eternal reproach and dishonour be it spoken, some persons of high rank and consequence in the kingdom availed themselves of that opportunity [the late recess], to become the emissaries of sedition, and to canvass popular clamour against the measure by the most shameless impositions on the ignorance and credulity of every man who would listen to them. The zealous Protestant was told, this is an insidious scheme of the British minister to deliver you up to the Papists, bound hand and foot. The Catholics were told, if you suffer this, there is an end to emancipation. The industrious farmer was told, if this takes place, there is an end of your lease, or if it should escape the grasp of your landlord, Mr. Pitt will take from you one-half of the

¹ *Parl. Deb.* of the 5th February, 1800, p. 147. J. Moore, Dublin.
² *Cast. Corr.* ii. 400.

profits of your farm. How will you like, if you have a profit of 50*l*. yearly on your farm, to pay 25*l*. to Mr. Pitt?"

Even the most seditious means of irritating the country were adopted. Inflammatory handbills were distributed among the yeomanry, calling on them to rise and save the country, and asking them whether 60,000 men with arms in their hands would tamely stand by and see the constitution of their country destroyed. The yeomanry were mostly Orangemen; fortunately that body was kept quiet by their Grand Master, Thomas Verner. On the 21st of January, 1800, Lord Cornwallis writes to the Duke of Portland, "Since my last communication to your Grace, every means have been taken by the anti-Unionists to inflame the minds of the people.... The most seditious and artful handbills are now in general circulation, calling upon the yeomanry, Orangemen, and Catholics to form one solid and indissoluble bond of opposition to the Union. And one of these productions is peculiarly addressed to the passions of the yeomanry by stating that no Government can wrest the Parliament from 60,000 armed and tried men."[1] On the 27th of the same month he again writes, "Every engine is at work to irritate the minds of the people, and to carry the opposition to the measure beyond constitutional bounds."[2] On the 31st, Lord Castlereagh writes,[3] "Every endeavour is made to excite the country. I understand from Lord Londonderry, who has just returned from the County Down, that the prevalent idea

[1] *Corn. Corr.* iii. 168.   [2] *Ib.* 173.   [3] *Ib.* iii. 175.

among the people is, that when the Parliament is taken away, *Irish* law will be at an end, and all their leases broken. They are told, to induce them to sign against the measure, that the reason so many gentlemen are for a union is, that they may new-let their estates at advanced rents." In February he again writes to the Duke of Portland,[1] "A not less formidable principle we have to contend against is the effect produced by their system of intimidation on the minds of our timid and lukewarm friends. The Opposition have shown their determination to rouse the disaffection of the country, and to hunt the people at the Government, and have not confined their efforts to the people alone. Both the yeomanry and militia are held forth to shake the constancy of our friends."[2]

A few examples of the conduct of the anti-Unionists will show us how far these gentlemen were willing to go along the path of sedition. Mr. Townley Balfour, afterwards member for Belturbet, at

[1] *Corn. Corr.* iii. 183.
[2] "I shall mention one laughable instance of the ingenuity of the anti-Unionists in this neighbourhood (Londonderry). The Catholics are told that by it (the Union) they will all be made Englishmen, and be obliged to go to church! The poor people are actually in terror of this metamorphosis. I will add another instance of the address of the party of which I have a perfect knowledge. When the petition from Tyrone to Parliament was in the hands of the manufacturers, the linen inspector for the county applied to the drapers in the market towns for lists of the weavers from whom they had purchased webs, and on being asked by a friend of mine for what purpose, bluntly answered, 'To make up the list of subscribers to the anti-Union petition.'"—Rev. Dr. Black to Lord Castlereagh, 26th April, 1800. *Cast. Corr.* iii. 287.

the County Louth meeting in 1799, moved the following resolution: "That if an Union be enacted by the legislature of this kingdom, either contrary to or without the advice of the assembled freeholders and burgesses, the submission of the people of Ireland thereto will be a matter of prudence and not of duty."[1] Sir William Worthington, commanding the Liberty Rangers, Dublin, ordered his corps to parade with the King's colour, but in lieu of the regimental colour a standard on which was inscribed, "For our King and the Constitution of Ireland."[2]

Mr. William Saurin was a King's Counsel, and commandant of the Lawyers' Infantry Corps, a body which included the barristers and attorneys of Dublin. This gentleman issued a regimental order directing his corps to meet "in their new regimentals" to discuss what was well known to be the question of Union. But as many members expressed their disapprobation of meeting as a military body to consider political matters, and of giving a warlike appearance to the opposition to that measure, Mr. Saurin was obliged to revoke his previous order and issue a new one, inviting the barristers only to attend, not as a military but as a civil body.[3] A few days later we find Mr. Saurin engaged in soliciting the officers of the different corps of yeomanry in Dublin to sign a paper stating their determination to lay down their arms in case the measure of Union should be brought forward.[4] Mr. Saurin was afterwards brought into Parliament in 1800

[1] *Corn. Corr.* iii. 97.
[3] *Ib.* iii. 5.
[2] *Ib.* iii. 29.
[4] *Ib.* iii. 29.

by Lord Downshire for his borough of Blessington, and was one of the most violent anti-Unionists in that assembly. Like so many others of the Opposition he was promoted after the Union, and became Attorney-General in 1807.[1]

Lord Downshire was the owner of vast estates, and possessed of enormous influence. He had created so many forty-shilling freeholders on his property that Wakefield describes it as a "warren" of such voters. His influence in his county was so great that Lord Cornwallis writes, in May, 1799, "Were Lord Downshire to come forward, we should have the county of Down unanimous."[2] This nobleman was Colonel of the Downshire Militia, which was then stationed in Carlow. In January, 1800, about the same time as the circular letter requesting petitions against the Union was signed

---

[1] There was hardly an opponent of the Union of any consequence who was not promoted or advanced after 1800. If this had been done in the case of the Unionists, calumny would have pointed at it as a proof of corruption. We give some of these promotions, &c.:

Plunket, Solicitor-General in 1803; Attorney-General, 1805.
George Ponsonby, Lord Chancellor, 1806.
W. B. Ponsonby, created Lord Ponsonby, 1806.
Foster (Speaker), Chancellor of the Exchequer, 1804, and pension, 5,038*l*.
His son, an office of 1,200*l*. a year.
Saurin, Attorney-General, 1807.
Bushe, Solicitor-General, 1805, till appointed C. J. 1822.
Prendergast Smyth, created Lord Kiltarton, 1810.
George Knox, a Lord of the Treasury, 1805.
Colonel Maxwell, do. 1810.
Curran, Goold, Burrowes, Ball, Bowes Daly, William Bagwell, Charles O'Hara, Barrington, A. Acheson, all promoted or advanced.

[2] *Cast. Corr.* ii. 319.

by him, and distributed through the country, Lord Downshire transmitted to his regiment the draft of a petition against that measure, with a request that the officers and soldiers should sign it. Between six and seven hundred signed it. The soldiers were in many cases ignorant of the contents of the paper presented to them for signature. Some imagined it was a petition in favour of the Union, others that it was a request *that the Union should not be carried out of the country.* The matter was closely investigated, and it was reported officially that Lord Downshire had acted as we have stated. He was dismissed his regiment, and from his office of Governor of the County Down; his name was also struck out of the Privy Council. The treatment of Lord Downshire by the Government was far too lenient. He ought to have been tried by court-martial for such a grave offence against the discipline of the army.[1] The crisis was a grave one, and Lord Cornwallis was so much alarmed by the seditious conduct of the anti-Unionists that on more than one occasion he pressed on the Government the necessity of despatching more troops to Ireland.[2]

But all the efforts of the anti-Unionists to irritate

[1] *Cast. Corr.* iii. 230-5. *Corn. Corr.* iii. 179.

[2] "Every exertion should be used on your side to send over without loss of time the whole or a part of the regular forces destined to serve in this country; and I think this step the more necessary as some of the Opposition are endeavouring to raise a popular clamour in Dublin and the adjacent counties" (18th Jan. 1800). "In this situation of affairs, and at this crisis, your Grace cannot be surprised at my again expressing an anxious hope for the speedy arrival of the reinforcement of troops which have been long expected" (27th Jan.).

and excite the people were made in vain. The country was satisfied, and therefore tranquil. Even Dublin had settled down. The successive accounts which Lord Cornwallis gives of the perfect quiet which prevailed in that city and throughout the country are both interesting and instructive. On the 22nd of April, 1800, he writes: "Dublin itself, although undoubtedly very averse to the Union, is in a state of more perfect tranquillity than it has ever before enjoyed;"[1] on the 13th of May, "The city is perfectly tranquil;"[2] on the 18th, "The country is perfectly quiet;"[3] on the 22nd, "The city is perfectly quiet, and has shown no sensation on the subject of union since the recommencement of business after the adjournment;"[4] on June 7th, "The greatest satisfaction is, that it occasions no agitation either in town or country;"[5] on the 3rd of July he speaks of "the quiet of the country at large on the subject, and the almost good-humoured indifference with which it is viewed in the metropolis."[6] And when he gave the Royal assent to the Act of Union, "There was not a murmur heard in the street, nor, I believe, an expression of ill-humour throughout the whole city of Dublin."[7] He again recurs to this subject in a letter to his friend Ross on the 16th of August, "Nothing can be more quiet than Dublin. In our procession through a part of the Liberties, in going from the Castle to St. Patrick's Cathedral at the Installation, the concourse of people was immense, and they all had cheerful countenances,

[1] *Corn. Corr.* iii. 229.   [2] *Ib.* iii. 238.   [3] *Ib.* iii. 235.
[4] *Ib.* iii. 239.   [5] *Ib.* iii. 249.   [6] *Ib.* iii. 270.
[7] *Ib.* iii. 285.

and when I passed they cried out, 'There he is,' 'That's he,' and often added, 'God bless him.'"[1]

For the country, to repeat the words of an anti-Unionist, had deserted the Opposition, and was satisfied with the terms of Union. For nearly two years the measure had been discussed in every household in the kingdom, in the newspapers and at county meetings. Both the communities which made up Ireland were content.[2] The dream of Molyneux was at last fulfilled; the wishes of the thinkers and writers of the country were accomplished. Ireland was received into partnership with Great Britain upon the equitable conditions of similarity of laws and privileges, and of national equality.

[1] *Corn. Corr.* iii. 288.

[2] "It may interest some of our readers to know that Lord Bristol, the once well-known Bishop of Derry, was in favour of the Union. He authorised the affixing of his signature to the declaration of the county of Londonderry."—*Belfast News Letter*, 8th Oct. 1799.

CHAPTER VI.

Sentiments of the Catholic community on the Union.—Support given to that measure by their peerage.—Their hierarchy.—Their inferior clergy.—Their laity.

THE position of the Irish Catholics before and at the time of the Union was peculiar, and deserves a short consideration. There is very little doubt that they would have preferred full emancipation, unaccompanied by a Union with England.[1] With their enormous preponderance of numbers, if the right of sitting in Parliament had been granted to them, they would soon have obtained a majority in the legislature. It is hard to say how far their wishes and ambition would have carried them on the opening of such an unbounded field. The first object of their attacks would naturally have been the Protestant Establishment, and from this they might have proceeded to the repeal of the Act of Settlement, and the reversal of the confiscations. These questions

---

[1] "For unquestionably no distinct description of persons had so interesting and strong an argument to ground their opposition upon as the body of Roman Catholics, who by the Union forfeited all the constitutional advantages of a most decided majority in an independent nation, to sink into an insignificant minority of the United Kingdom."—Plowden, vol. ii. pt. ii. 980.

alone would have led to civil war, perhaps to separation and a fresh conquest by England. For the disturbance could not have been limited to Ireland alone. A Protestant England and Catholic Ireland, united under a Protestant King, who by his coronation oath was bound to maintain the Protestant religion, would have been a political monster, whose life must indeed have been but of short duration.

On the other hand, the Irish Catholics were well aware that full emancipation would not be granted to them by an Irish Protestant Parliament as long as it could be refused with safety. They knew that the Protestants were acquainted with the danger of their own position, and that they dreaded the growing power and preponderance of the Catholics. Flood asked in the House of Commons the pertinent question, to which no answer could be given: "If you grant equal rights to the Catholics, how can the constitution be maintained?" To whom then were the Catholics to look? Under whose banner were they to range themselves? One party among the anti-Unionists, that known as Charlemonts, was resolute against any further concession, and sincerely believed that the admission of Catholics to political power would be fatal to the stability of the country. The other party, led by Grattan, was in favour of their full and immediate emancipation without a Union. The Catholics were sagacious enough to see that Grattan's position was untenable. Though they were grateful to him for his eloquent advocacy of their claims, they were often disturbed and repelled by his inconsistencies, inconsistencies so great that they are almost unintelligible.

Grattan was for hurrying on emancipation, yet he was the unflinching champion of Protestant ascendency. "These being my principles," he writes in 1793, in his answer to an address from the citizens of Dublin, " and the Protestant interest my first object, you may judge that I shall never assent to any measure tending to shake the security of property in the kingdom, or to subvert the Protestant ascendency."[1] Grattan tells us that he loved the Catholics, yet he allowed himself to speak of their religion in a manner, which if it were done at the present day would be justly reprobated. "In Ireland," says he, "as connected with England, the indulgence we wish to give to Catholics can never be injurious to the Protestant religion. That religion is the religion of the State, and will become the religion of Catholics if severity does not prevent them. Bigotry may survive persecution, but it can never survive toleration."[2] This extraordinary statement is perfectly unqualified by the context, and furnishes perhaps the only example in the world of a public man declaring openly that the convictions of four millions of his fellow-subjects rested on obstinacy or bigotry. Outside the pages of Partridge's almanacs it would be difficult to find such a combination of the folly of prophecy, and the ignoring of patent facts.

It was clear to the Catholics that there was no safety to be expected from the leadership of Grattan. Under these circumstances they began, though they were slow at moving, to turn their eyes to the English Government—

[1] Grattan's *Miscel. Works*, 289, quoted by Lecky, note iv. 386.
[2] Speech on the Catholic question, 20th Feb. 1782.

that Government which they had long looked upon, not as their oppressor, but as their protector, and with whom they had always sympathised much more strongly than with their native Parliament.[1] They began to ground their hopes on an Imperial Parliament where their case might be considered in an unprejudiced tribunal free from local feelings and petty jealousies. They saw, on the one hand, that emancipation would not without a contest be conceded by their domestic Parliament on account of the danger to the Protestant Establishment, and the fear of weakening Protestant titles. And that, on the other, it might be safely granted by a united Parliament without danger to the constitution or probability of internal dissensions. These motives determined them to accept Union, accompanied, they hoped, with emancipation, for they believed that emancipation without Union seemed scarcely possible. And having chosen one side of the alternative, they gave it their warm and hearty approbation. They were willing to support it without raising the question of their admission to Parliament. Nay, they were actually opposed to starting this consideration lest it should render the measure of Union more difficult.[2] They trusted that the Imperial Parliament would dispassionately consider their claims, a thing which their leaders declared the Irish Parliament was not capable of doing, and that it would at a proper time allow them every privilege consistent with the constitution.[3] Without a single direct promise in their favour, though not without expectation of future concessions, the Irish Catholics took up the

[1] Lecky, iv. 462.   [2] *Corn. Corr.* iii. 8.   [3] *Ib.*

measure of Union and lent it their hearty concurrence. And it is remarkable that some of their foremost men hesitated to do this openly lest they should injure the cause to which they had devoted themselves. We shall subsequently see that the Catholic Archbishop of Tuam for this reason delayed for many days to affix his signature to a resolution in favour of the Union. And that the Bishop of Meath, though he signed afterwards, for the same reason did not at first sign the declaration of the county of Meath.

In December, 1798, Lord Cornwallis tells us that the Catholics were in favour of a Union; of this he was assured by the Catholic Archbishop of Dublin and Lords Fingall and Kenmare.[1] The Catholics appear to have hesitated, or to have feared to come forward for some time.[2] In July, 1799, Lord Cornwallis writes again : " If I may confide in the accounts I receive, the measure is working very favourably in the south. Within these few days the Catholics have shown a disposition to depart from their line of neutrality and to support the measure. Those of the city of Waterford have sent up a very strong declaration in favour of Union, at the same time expressing a hope that it will lead to the accomplishment of their emancipation as they term it, but not looking to it as a preliminary. The Catholics of Kilkenny have agreed to a similar

[1] *Corn. Corr.* iii. 8.
[2] At a meeting at Lord Fingall's, 15th Dec. 1798, "The general opinion of the meeting was that the Catholics as such ought not to deliberate on the Union as a question of Empire, but only as it might affect their own peculiar interests."—Dr. Troy to Lord Castlereagh. *Cast. Corr.* ii. 61.

declaration; and as the clergy of that church, particularly the superiors, countenance the measure, it is likely to extend itself."[1] In November 1799, he writes: "The Union is, I trust, making progress; the great body of the people in general, and of the Catholics in particular, are decidedly for it."[2]

But we are not left merely to the evidence of strangers to the Catholic body. In December 1798, the Archbishop of Dublin and Lords Kenmare and Fingall declared they had no hope in the Irish Parliament, and that they looked forward to a united Parliament to grant them the privileges they desired.[3] In September 1799, Dr. Moylan, Bishop of Cork, writes to Sir J. C. Hippesley,[4] a well-known and warm friend of the Catholics: "The Roman Catholics in general are avowedly for the measure. In the south, where they are the most numerous, they have declared in its favour, and I am sure they will do the same in the other parts of the kingdom unless overawed (as I know they are in some counties) by the dread of the powerful faction that opposes it. In this city (Dublin), where the outcry against it has been so very violent, it is becoming every day less unpopular, and I am persuaded that the Roman Catholic inhabitants will in time testify their approbation of it.[5] In the same month the Archbishop of

---

[1] Lord Cornwallis to Duke of Portland.—*Cast. Corr.* ii. 351.
[2] *Corn. Corr.* iii. 143.   [3] *Ib.* 8.
[4] It was this gentleman who was the means of obtaining from George III. a pension of 4,000*l.* for Cardinal Stuart, the last of that unhappy family, who so pathetically described himself on his medals, *Rex Britt., &c. Dei gratia sed non hominum voluntate.*
[5] *Cast. Corr.* ii. 399.

Tuam writes to the Archbishop of Dublin : " I have had an opportunity, in the course of the parochial visitation of this diocese, which is nearly finished, of observing how little averse the public mind is to that measure·; and I have also had an opportunity of acquiring the strongest conviction that this measure alone can restore harmony and happiness to our unhappy country."[1] In October, 1799, the Archbishop of Dublin writes: " You will observe, by our public papers, that the question of Union is daily gaining ground. The Catholics are coming forward in different parts in favour of the measure, which the generality of them consider as their only protection against a faction seemingly intent on their defamation or destruction."[2]

It was asserted by O'Connell that the Irish Catholics did not assent to the Act of Union. This assertion has been repeated by declaimers who are impatient of laborious research and follow blindly without inquiry. On this statement an argument has been founded that as the Catholics did not assent to the Union they are not bound by it. It therefore becomes necessary to examine the assertion, and at the risk of length and repetition to consider it with some minuteness.

There is not the slightest foundation for the assertion. On the contrary, all the evidence goes to show irresistibly that the Catholics did assent to the measure of Union ; and that their peerage, their episcopacy, their inferior clergy, and their laity gave to it their hearty concurrence and co-operation.

[1] *Cast. Corr.* ii. 386. This diocese includes nearly all Mayo and portions of Galway and Roscommon. [2] *Ib.* ii. 420.

The Catholics of Ireland assented to the Union by the majority of their representatives in Parliament. To say that that assent was not binding on them, and is not binding on their successors, because the Catholics had not then the right of sitting in the legislature, would be hazardous and would prove too much. For such an argument would prove that the Scotch Union was not and is not binding on the Scotch and English Catholics. Members of this communion were numerous in both those countries, and the Highlands were in great part Catholic at the time of the Scotch Union. These bodies had neither the privilege of the franchise, nor were they represented in Parliament; yet what jurist would venture to argue that they themselves were not bound, and that their descendants are not bound, by the Act of Union and by the decision of the Parliaments of their countries as then established by law? The Irish Catholics at the time of their Union were much more favourably situated than were those of England and Scotland in 1707, or even 120 years later. They were fully represented in their native Parliament, or rather, they were enormously over-represented when compared with the electoral body of either England or Scotland.

The validity, therefore, of the Union and of the proceedings of 1800 may be rested on the assent of the Catholics given by their representatives, and on the strict and recognised principles of the Constitution, which declare that the Parliament for the time being is competent to bind every subject whether represented or not. Any other doctrine is unsettling and hazardous. But we need not stop here, for it can be proved that the private wishes and hopes of the Catholic community corresponded to the public assent given by them constitutionally in Parliament.

The Irish Catholic peers were strongly in favour of a Union. In the beginning of the year 1800 this body had occasion to write to Lord Cornwallis respecting a claim which they were then urging as to a right of their order. They thus express their sentiments on the subject of a Union : " The Catholic peers, therefore, my Lord, do not wish by any means to press at this time a claim which shall be considered as likely to embarrass the great national measure now depending, from which they expect such benefits for their country at large, and looking forward with the most unbounded confidence to the magnanimity, liberality, and sound policy of the future Imperial legislature, venture to promise to themselves and the whole Catholic body many more considerable and extensive advantages." [1]

The entire Catholic episcopacy of Ireland, consisting of four Archbishops and nineteen Bishops, for three bishoprics were then vacant, was favourable to the Union.

In 1799, the English Government made a State provision for the Catholic church in Scotland. How gratefully this provision was received, may be gathered from the following extract from a letter signed by two of the Scotch Vicars Apostolic,[2] George Hay, Bishop of Daulia

[1] *Corn. Corr.* iii. 204. The letter is dated 7th March, 1800.
[2] There were then no Catholic bishops in Scotland taking titles from Scotch localities. See *Series Episcoporum Eccles. Cathol.*, by Bonifacius Gams, O.S.B.

and John Chisholm, Bishop of Diocæsarea. "You will easily conceive how great a consolation this intelligence gave us, to see ourselves and our clergy, by this singular assistance from our generous benefactors raised to a comfortable situation from almost absolute poverty. But what greatly enhanced the favour was the amiable and endearing manner in which his lordship[1] communicated the intelligence to us."[2] In the same year the Irish episcopacy was in treaty with Lord Castlereagh, the unwavering friend of the Catholics, for a similar provision for the Irish clergy. We know this from the resolutions of the Irish Bishops given below,[3] and from a

[1] Lord Advocate of Scotland.
[2] *Cast. Corr.* ii. 332.
[3] "At a meeting of the Roman Catholic prelates, held at Dublin on the 17th, 18th, and 19th January, 1799, to deliberate on a proposal from Government of an independent provision for the Roman Catholic clergy of Ireland, under certain regulations not incompatible with their doctrines, discipline, or just influence, it was admitted that a provision through Government for the Roman Catholic clergy of this kingdom, competent and secured, ought to be thankfully accepted.

"That in the appointment of the prelates of the Roman Catholic religion to the vacant sees within the kingdom, such interference of Government as may enable it to be satisfied of the loyalty of the person appointed is just and ought to be agreed to.

"That to give the principle its full operation, without infringing the discipline of the Roman Catholic Church, or diminishing the religious influence which prelates of that church ought justly to possess over their respective flocks, the following regulations seem necessary :—

"1. In the vacancy of a see, the clergy of the diocese to recommend as usual a candidate to the prelates of the ecclesiastical province who elect him, or any other they may think more worthy, by a majority of suffrages. In the case of equality of suffrages, the metropolitan or senior prelate to have the casting vote.

letter of the Catholic Archbishop of Dublin, dated the 9th
of February in this year. On that day the Archbishop

" 2. In the election of a metropolitan, if the provincial prelates do
not agree within two months after the vacancy, the senior prelate
shall forthwith invite the surviving metropolitans to the election,
in which each will have a vote. In the equality of suffrages, the
presiding metropolitan to have a casting vote.

" 3. In these elections the majority of suffrages must be *ultra
medietatem*, as the canons require, or must consist of the suffrages of
more than half the electors.

" 4. The candidates so elected to be presented by the president of
the election to Government, which within one month after such
presentation will transmit the name of the said candidate, if no
objection be made against him, for appointment to the holy see, or
return the said name to the president of the election for such
transmission as may be agreed on.

" 5. If Government have any proper objection against such candidates, the president of the election will be informed thereof within
one month after presentation, who in that case will convene the
electors to the election of another candidate.

" Agreeably to the discipline of the Roman Catholic Church, these
regulations can have no effect without the sanction of the holy see,
which sanction the Roman Catholic prelates of this kingdom shall,
as soon as may be, use their endeavours to procure. The prelates
are satisfied that the nomination of parish priests, with a certifi-
cate of their having taken the oath of allegiance, be certified to
Government.

" RICHARD O'REILLY, R.C.A.B. Armagh
" J. S. TROY, R.C.A.B. Dublin.
" EDWARD DILLON, R.C.A.B. Tuam.
" THOMAS BRAY, R.C.A.B. Cashel.
" P. J. PLUNKETT, R.C.B. Meath.
" J. MOYLAN, R.C.B. Cork.
" DANIEL DELANY, R.C.B. Kildare.
" EDMUND FRENCH, R.C.B. Elphin.
" JAMES CAULFIELD, R.C.B. Ferns.
" JOHN CRUISE, R.C.B. Ardagh.

—*Grattan's Life*, v. 57. Wakefield's *Ireland*, ii. 514.

writes: "Most of my brethren lately assembled here are gone home. As the measure of providing for our clergy seems connected with the question of Union which has been prematurely opposed in our Commons' House, the former must be postponed until the other be coolly considered in Parliament. Previous to the separation of my brethren, certain preliminary points were agreed upon and sent by me to Lord Castlereagh, who expressed his approbation of them, and probably sent them to the Duke of Portland. They are not to be made public until the business be concluded. Meantime, Dr. O'Reilly, of Armagh, and Plunkett, of Meath, in conjunction with me, are authorised by our brethren to treat with Lord Castlereagh on the subject, when he may think it expedient to resume it."[1]

If the fact that the Irish episcopacy was engaged in a secret treaty with Government for a State provision for the Catholic clergy, which provision was only to take effect in the event of a Union, be not sufficient evidence that this body was in favour of that measure, we have other and exceedingly strong evidence of their approval of it. The literature of private letters and newspapers is fleeting and evanescent, but still undeniable proofs survive, and it is from such sources that we know that the four Catholic Archbishops were strongly in favour of the Union.

As to Dr. O'Reilly, Archbishop of Armagh, and Primate of Ireland, the Archbishop of Tuam tells us

---

[1] Dr. Troy to Sir J. C. Hippisley, *Cast. Corr.* ii. 171.

that this prelate advised him to sign a resolution in favour of a Union.[1]

The Archbishop of Dublin was from the first a most strenuous supporter of the Union. Many of his letters survive exhorting his brethren to sign themselves, and to obtain the signatures of others to declarations in favour of that measure. Thus, in July, 1799, he advised the Archbishop of Tuam to sign a declaration in favour of the Union, and his brother of Tuam writes back to him in answer to his exhortation, "Supported, however, by your sanction and that of Dr. O'Reilly, I think I may venture to request of your lordship to sign it for me."[2]

On July 1st, 1799, the Archbishop of Cashel writes to the Archbishop of Dublin : "As far as I understand the measure, it will be productive of substantial benefits to both countries, and therefore it meets my good wishes and shall have the whole of my little mite of assistance, but with due attention to the necessary cautions and hints so wisely suggested by Lord Castlereagh."[3]

On September 1st, 1799, the Archbishop of Tuam writes: "I feel myself each day less shy of publicly declaring my sentiments and wishes relative to the Union. I have had an opportunity, in the course of the parochial visitation of this diocese which is nearly finished, of observing how little averse the public mind is to that measure ; and I have also had an opportunity

---

[1] Dr. Dillon to Dr. Troy, *Cast. Corr.* ii. 347.   [2] *Ib.* ii. 347.
[3] The Archbishop of Cashel to Dr. Troy, *ib.* ii. 344.

of acquiring the strongest conviction that this measure alone can restore harmony and happiness to our unhappy country."[1]

Such are the opinions of the four Archbishops of Ireland. We now come to the Bishops.

Dr. Plunkett, Bishop of Meath, writes on the 29th October, 1799, "For my part I will heartily join the Roman Catholics of Meath the instant they will show a disposition to declare in favour of a Union."[2] In February, 1800, this Bishop signed the declaration of the county of Meath in favour of that measure.[3] A few days later he and his Vicar-General, Dr. Mullaly, signed a similar declaration of the county Westmeath.[4]

In September, 1799, Dr. Cruise, Bishop of Ardagh and Clonmacnoise, presided at a meeting of the Catholics of the county Longford, which drew up an address to Lord Cornwallis in favour of "an incorporate Union with Great Britain," and was the first to sign it "for self and clergy."[5] The united dioceses of this bishop contained thirty-nine parish priests and thirteen curates.[6]

On the 28th of July, 1799, Dr. Bellew, Bishop of Killala, presided at a meeting of the Catholics of the Baronies of Tyrawley and Tireragh, which declared for

---

[1] Dr. Dillon to Dr. Troy, *Cast. Corr.* ii. 386.
[2] *Ib.* ii. 437.
[3] Advertisement, *Belfast News Letter*, 4th March, 1800.
[4] *Ib.* advert. 11th March, 1800.
[5] *Ib.* advert. 1st Oct. 1799.
[6] See this bishop's report on the state of his diocese, *Cast. Corr.* 114.

a Legislative Union.¹ This Bishop also signed in this month the declaration of the county Mayo in favour of a Union.²

Dr. Lanigan, Bishop of Ossory, was the first on a committee appointed by the Catholics of Kilkenny, to draw up a declaration in favour of a Legislative Union. The meeting took place on the 9th of July, 1799, and was unanimous. The declaration was drawn up and forwarded to Lord Cornwallis on the 19th of the same month.³

On the 22nd September, 1799, Dr. Caulfield, Bishop of Ferns, presided at a meeting of the Catholics of Wexford and its vicinity, which drew up an address to Lord Cornwallis in favour of "an incorporation of both legislatures." This address was signed by upwards of 3,000 persons.⁴

In January, 1800, Dr. French, Bishop of Elphin, presided at a meeting of the Catholic clergy of this diocese which drew up an address to Lord Cornwallis in favour of a Legislative Union.⁵ This diocese contained fifty-nine parish priests and twenty-two curates.⁶

In September, 1799, Dr. Moylan, Bishop of Cork, writes: "Nothing, in my opinion, will more effectually tend to lay those disgraceful and scandalous party feuds and dissensions, and restore peace and harmony

---

¹ Advert. *Belfast News Letter*, 23rd Aug. 1799.
² *Ib.* advert. 19th July, 1799.   ³ *Ib.* advert. 10th Sept. 1799.
⁴ *Ib.* advert. 19th Nov. 1799.   ⁵ *Ib.* advert. 14th Jan. 1800.
⁶ See this bishop's report on the state of his diocese, *Cast. Corr.* iv. 166.

amongst us, than the great measure in contemplation of the Legislative Union and incorporation of this kingdom with Great Britain."[1] On the 28th July, 1800, the Bishop writes again: "The great question of Legislative Union is, thank God, most happily decided. The manner in which Lord Castlereagh has conducted that important measure is highly honourable to his lordship, and evinces the most extensive abilities. May the Almighty grant him health and length of days to consolidate the good work, and to see the advantages realised which are expected eventually to accrue from it to this most distracted country."[2]

Dr. Delany, Bishop of Kildare and Leighlin, was in favour of the Union. Sir J. C. Hippisley writes, on the 27th February, 1799: "Mr. Macdonald, the chaplain of the Glengarry regiment, showed me this morning a letter from the titular Bishop Delany, who mentions Dr. Troy[3] having read my letter to the assembly of Catholic bishops before they left Dublin. Delany speaks highly in favour of the Union, but says the excesses committed on many of the Catholic clergy still obtain."[4]

We have already seen that Dr. Lennan, Bishop of Dromore, lent his aid to the Union, and that in answer to Dr. Troy's request for his assistance, this Bishop and the Catholics of Newry re-elected the Chancellor of the Exchequer, a strong Unionist, against Mr. Ball, an able and eloquent anti-Unionist.

In July, 1799, Dr. Sugrue, Bishop of the united

[1] *Cast. Corr.* ii. 399.
[2] *Ib.* iii. 364.
[3] Archbishop of Dublin.
[4] *Cast. Corr.* ii. 188.

dioceses of Ardfert and Aghadoe—generally called the diocese of Kerry, signed the declaration of the county of Kerry in favour of a Union.[1]

In September, 1799, Dr. O'Donnell, Bishop of Derry, signed the declaration in favour of a Union made by the city of Londonderry.[2]

In the same month, Dr. McMahon, Bishop of Killaloe, signed the declaration of the city and county of Limerick in favour of a Legislative Union.[3]

In December, 1799, Dr. Coyle, Bishop of Raphoe, signed the Donegal declaration in favour of a Union.[4]

Dr. V. Bodkin, for many years the agent of the secular[5] Irish Bishops at Rome, writes from Galway, in February, 1799: "I am far from thinking the Union lost." (This was after the first debate in the Commons.) "A little time will rally and bring back the disheartened and disaffected. It is the only means left to save from ruin and destruction that poor and infatuated Ireland."[6]

Three of the Irish Bishoprics were vacant at this time. Achonry, from which Dr. Egan had been translated to Tuam, and had died almost immediately; Kilmacduagh and Kilfenora, which Dr. Concannen had

---

[1] Advert. *Belfast News Letter*, 19th July, 1799.
[2] *Ib.* 24th Sept. 1799.   [3] *Ib.* 1st Oct. 1799.
[4] *Ib.* 20th Dec. 1799.
[5] There were two regulars, bishops in Ireland, Dr. Troy, Archbishop of Dublin, and Dr. McMahon, Bishop of Killaloe, both Dominicans. Dr. Concannen, also a Dominican, had been shortly before appointed Bishop of Kilmacduagh and Kilfenora, but he resigned and returned to Rome.
[6] *Cast. Corr.* ii. 188.

resigned; and Kilmore, which remained vacant till some time in 1800.[1]

Thus, out of a hierarchy of four Archbishops and nineteen Bishops, we have the four Archbishops, thirteen Bishops, and the agent of the secular Bishops, all declaring by words and deeds that the Union was necessary to save Ireland. When we read these statements and remember the unity of action which the Irish Catholic Episcopacy has invariably observed in every political movement; and when we further remember that this body was then in treaty with the Government for a State provision for themselves and their clergy, it is impossible to come to any other conclusion than that the Catholic Episcopacy unanimously supported the Union publicly and privately, by exhortation as well as by example. The unanimity of their support is the more remarkable, because the timid members among them were afraid that their public assistance would endanger the measure. "I am certain," writes the Archbishop of Tuam to the Archbishop of Dublin, on the 9th July, 1799, apologising for his delay in signing a declaration in favour of the Union, "that our bishops could more effectually promote any great measure which Government may adopt for the benefit of our country by not appearing so publicly to take an active part in the present political contest. These considerations, together with the difficulties in which, by such a precedent, I should probably involve some of our brethren more immediately exposed to the wrath of our enemies than I am, have left me wavering and uncertain

[1] *Series Episcoporum Eccles. Cathol.*

for many days. Supported, however, by your sanction and that of Dr. O'Reilly I think I may venture to request of your lordship to sign it for me. My vicar-general and dean have already signed."[1] To a similar effect the Archbishop of Cashel had written to the same prelate a few days before. "If we act in any ostensible capacity in the business of Union either by a personal signature to an address in favour of it, or otherwise, in my humble opinion, instead of serving the cause we may injure it."[2]

As for the sentiments of the inferior clergy—we have already seen that Dr. Cruise, Bishop of Ardagh and Clonmacnoise signed, on behalf of the clergy of these dioceses, the declaration of the Catholics of the county Longford in favour of the Union, and that Dr. French, Bishop of Elphin, presided at a meeting of the clergy of this diocese which drew up an address to Lord Cornwallis. In June, 1799, Lord Altamont writes from Westport in reference to the county Mayo declaration in favour of a Union: "The priests have all offered to sign."[3] In January, 1800, the clergy was one of the three constituent parts of the Kilkenny county meeting which declared in favour of a Union. The name of the parish priest is the first on the committee of the Catholics of Waterford who addressed Lord Cornwallis.[4] The Rev. Charles Doran, P.P., was the chairman of the Catholics of five parishes in Kildare and King's County which declared for the Union.[5] The Rev. James Martin, P.P., was the chairman of the Dundalk Catholics who

[1] *Cast. Corr.* ii. 347.   [2] *Ib.* ii. 344.   [3] *Ib.* ii. 327.
[4] *Belfast News Letter,* 23rd Aug. 1799.   [5] *Ib.* 13th Sept. 1799.

addressed Lord Cornwallis.[1] The Rev. W. Chapman, P.P., presided at the meeting of the Catholics of New Ross and its neighbourhood who also addressed Lord Cornwallis.[2] The name of the Rev. P. Quin, P.P., heads the declaration made by the Catholics of Lower Cregan.[3] Parish priests signed freely the seventy-four declarations and petitions in favour of the Union made in all parts of Ireland. When we recollect that these were the times of Protestant ascendency, it is astonishing to find so many of the Catholic clergy venturing to support publicly a political measure which caused so much excitement, and appealed to so many passions. It is not to be expected that letters written by private individuals should be preserved, but one survives which will give an idea of the universal favour which the Union met with from the class of the writer, and also from the Catholic laity. The letter is dated the 17th January, 1800, and is addressed by the Rev. H. Dowling to Lord Castlereagh. The following is an extract: "Though an obscure individual, yet extremely anxious lest the intemperate conduct of some of my brethren in communion (for I am a Catholic clergyman) should impress Government with an opinion that the sentiments of the generality of that communion were in unison with theirs, I have taken the liberty thus to intrude myself on your Lordship, in order to assure you that I and thousands of my brethren in the country parts of Ireland, whose sentiments I speak, feel exceedingly indignant at the rash and intem-

[1] *Belfast News Letter*, 15th Oct. 1799.   [2] *Ib.* 29th Oct.
[3] *Ib.* 17th January, 1800.

perate conduct of the Dublin Catholics on a late—or, rather a present—occasion. I mean, relative to the business of a legislative union. In the country parts of the kingdom we only wait to be called upon in order to declare our decided opinion in favour of that measure."[1]

If further evidence be required as to the support which the Catholic episcopacy and clergy gave to the Union, it is forthcoming. On the 15th of January, 1800, in the House of Commons, Grattan, irritated by the assistance which that body lent to the measure, described the Catholic clergy as " a band of prostituted men engaged in the service of Government."[2] And Plowden, a Catholic, tells us " it may indeed be said that a very great preponderancy in favour of the Union existed in the Catholic body, particularly in their nobility, gentry, and clergy."[3]

Nor were the Catholic laity a whit behind their clergy in giving their support to the Union.

On the 28th of June, 1799, the Catholics of Waterford and its vicinity presented an address to Lord Cornwallis in favour of a Legislative Union.[4]

On the 28th of July the Catholics of the Baronies of Tyrawley and Tireragh, situated in the counties of Mayo and Sligo, with their Bishop in the chair, passed a resolution unanimously in favour of a Legislative Union.[5]

[1] *Cast. Corr.* iii. 226.
[2] *Hist. of the Debates of 15th Jan.* J. Milliken, Dublin, 1800. *Baron Smith's Letter to Grattan,* p. 69.
[3] *Review of the State of Ireland,* vol. ii. pt. ii. 979.
[4] Advert. *Belfast News Letter,* 23rd Aug. [5] *Ib.*

In August, the Catholics of the city of Cork addressed Lord Cornwallis in favour of this measure.[1]

On the 22nd September, at a meeting of the Catholics of Wexford and its vicinity, their Bishop in the chair, a similar address was drawn up unanimously.[2]

On the 31st of July, the Catholics of the towns of Tipperary and Cahir, and their vicinity, drew up an address to Lord Cornwallis in favour of a Union.[3]

On the 9th of July, 1799, at a meeting of the Catholics of the city of Kilkenny, a declaration in favour of a Legislative Union was unanimously adopted.[4]

On the 1st of September, the Catholics of the parishes of Monasterevan, Lacka, Harristown, Nurney, and Ballybracken, in the counties of Kildare and King's County, unanimously adopted the declaration of the Catholics of Waterford in favour of the Union.[5]

In August, 1799, the Catholics of the county of Longford, the Bishop of Ardagh and Clonmacnoise in the chair, drew up unanimously an address to Lord Cornwallis in favour of a Union.[6]

In October, the Catholics of Dundalk, the parish priest in the chair, addressed Lord Cornwallis in favour of that measure.[7]

In the same month, the Catholics of New Ross and its vicinity, the parish priest in the chair, drew up a similar address.[8]

In January, 1800, the Catholics of Lower Cregan,

---

[1] Advert. *Belfast News Letter*, 23rd Aug.   [2] *Ib.* 19th Nov.
[3] *Ib.* 3rd Sept.   [4] *Ib.* 13th Sept.   [5] *Ib.*
[6] *Ib.* 1st Oct.   [7] *Ib.* 15th Oct.   [8] *Ib.* 29th Oct.

county Armagh, passed a declaration in favour of the Union.¹

In the same month, the Catholic "gentlemen, clergy, and freeholders" of the county of Kilkenny declared "their most heartfelt approbation of the intended measure of a Legislative Union between this kingdom and Great Britain."²

In this month also, the Catholics of the city of Limerick,"with one dissentient voice," drew up an address to Lord Cornwallis in favour of a Union.³

In this month, 1,500 Catholics of the county of Roscommon forwarded their signatures, separately from the Protestants, to the declaration in favour of the Union made by that county.⁴

Finally, Plowden tells us that the Catholics of the county of Leitrim also came forward and addressed in favour of that measure. But he does not mention the date; he merely says that the address was signed by 1,836 persons.⁵

In January, 1799, Lord Kenmare informed Lord Cornwallis "that the part of the Opposition which was the least indisposed to the Catholics had sent to the principal persons of that religion in the metropolis, to assure them that, if they would present a petition against the Union, a motion should be made, as soon as the question of Union was disposed of, in favour of Catholic emancipation." ⁶ Notwithstanding this offer and the efforts of the anti-Unionists, the Catholics stood firm.

¹ Advert. *Belfast News Letter*, 17th Jan. 1800.
² *Ib.* 11th Feb. 1800.   ³ *Ib.*   ⁴ *Cast. Corr.* iii. 222.
⁵ *Review, App.* 323.   ⁶ *Corn. Corr.* iii. 52.

Not a single petition against the Union was presented by that body to the King, Lord-Lieutenant, or either House of Parliament.

Theobald McKenna, formerly Secretary to the Catholic Committee, then a well-known body acting for the whole of the Irish Catholics, wrote two pamphlets in favour of the Union.[1]

Plowden informs us of some of the reasons which determined the Irish Catholics to give such support to the Union. "The severities and indignities practised upon them [the Catholics] after the rebellion by many of the Orange body, and the offensive affected confusion and use of the terms *papist* and *rebel* produced fresh soreness in the minds of many; the pointed recollection of the long suffering of their body from their own legislature, and the grateful sense of the benefits they had received from the parental tenderness of their Sovereign, after the indignant rejection and contumely of the Irish Parliament; all naturally tended to inspire the Catholics with plenary confidence and attachment to the Marquis Cornwallis and this favourite measure of his Government."[2]

---

[1] *Memoirs on the Projected Union* and *Constitutional Objections to the Government of Ireland by a Separate Legislature.*

[2] *Review*, vol. ii. pt. ii. 980.

CHAPTER VII.

Union debates of 1800.

WHEN the Irish Parliament met on the 15th of January, 1800, the battle was practically won. The country was content with the terms of Union offered. Though the Government had not yet fully revealed the conditions of the proposed treaty between the two kingdoms, yet sufficient had leaked out to satisfy both the communities which made up the people of Ireland. Lord Castlereagh had communicated the outlines of the Government plan to the principal men of the country, and from these the suggested arrangements had transpired to the public in general. A marked change had come over the feeling of the country as early as April, 1799, when it became known that every consideration would be shown to those classes whose interests were likely to be affected by the measure. And when the actual terms of the Union were explained by Lord Castlereagh in the House of Commons on the 5th of February, they were received with general satisfaction. Mr., afterwards Baron Smith, writing at the very moment of their explanation, thus speaks of them: "The splendour of these terms supersedes all inferior arguments for union; and the man must be more phlegmatic than

I desire to be, who can listen to them, and withhold his admiration. By these, as if the British constitution were not of itself a boon worthy of our acceptance, advantages are secured in commerce and finance equalling the fondest hopes we could have formed, and almost exceeding the powers of calculation. Upon a principle, the fairness of which is beyond dispute, the contribution of Ireland will be proportioned to its ability, and that ability be measured by an accurate criterion; nor will any power be given to the Imperial Parliament of altering or revising this principle in any respect; but merely of insuring its future application, and making the ability of Ireland the eternal and invariable standard of her contribution."

On the first day of the meeting of Parliament, a speech from the throne was delivered by Lord Cornwallis, in which no reference was made to a Union, because that measure was intended to be made the subject of a distinct communication. After an address had been moved and seconded in the Commons, Sir Lawrence Parsons wishing to take the sense of the House on the question of Union, moved an amendment, declaring a desire for the continuance of British connection, and the wish for the preservation of an independent resident Parliament. A debate ensued, in which Lord Castlereagh, the Right Honourable David Latouche, the Attorney-General, and the Chancellor of the Exchequer were the principal speakers on the side of the Government; Plunket, Grattan, Bushe, George Ponsonby, and Sir John Parnell, on the side of the Opposition.

The speech of David Latouche, the head of a great banking firm, made a strong impression on the House.

He declared that, in his opinion, a Union would promote peace and order in the country; that it would benefit both the landed and commercial interests of Great Britain and Ireland; and that it would open the way to the satisfaction of the claims of the Catholics.

A difference was discernible between the opinions of the mover of the amendment and several of his supporters. The drift of Sir L. Parsons' arguments was that a Legislative Union with Great Britain would be at all times and under all possible circumstances disadvantageous to Ireland, whilst J. C. Beresford, Lord Cole, and the Right Honourable George Ogle admitted that cases might occur where a union would be desirable. Ogle's speech annoyed the Opposition greatly. He said he disapproved of the conduct of many of the anti-Unionists, but that on such a question he would co-operate with them, "and though I shall never connect myself with such persons, yet on this ground I will co-operate with any man, laudable or not, with every man, with virtues or without them, whether he acts conscientiously or factiously; I will avail myself of every man who defends the constitution."[1]

At about seven o'clock in the morning, when Mr. Egan had risen, and was dilating on the exertions of Mr. Grattan in the settlement of 1782, the latter gentleman entered the House, looking ill, and supported by his two friends, W. B. Ponsonby and Arthur Moore. Grattan had been elected the night before for Wicklow, having purchased his seat for 2,400*l.*[2] The editor of the Cornwallis

---
[1] *Hist. of the Debates*, p. 27. Milliken, Dublin, 1800.
[2] *Corn. Corr.* iii. 161.

Correspondence says that the fortunate moment for his entrance had been watched for, and that the scene was well got up, but that the trick was too palpable, and produced little effect. Grattan was able, however, to deliver a very long and inflammatory speech, which did more harm than good to his party. It was in this speech that Grattan, angry with the Catholic clergy for their support of the Union, called that body "a band of prostituted men engaged in the service of Government." He was effectively answered by Corry, and the amendment was rejected, at ten o'clock in the morning of the 16th, by a majority of forty-two, ninety-six voting for the amendment and a hundred and thirty-eight against it.

On the 5th of February, Lord Castlereagh informed the House that he had a message to it from the Lord-Lieutenant, which he read. The message intimated that the Viceroy had the commands of the King to lay before the House for its consideration the resolutions of the British Parliament, "proposing and recommending a complete and entire union between Great Britain and Ireland, to be established by the mutual consent of both Parliaments, founded on equal and liberal principles, on the similarity of laws, constitution, and government, and on a sense of mutual interests and affection." Lord Castlereagh then proceeded to open up and explain at great length the proposed plan of the Union, and concluded by moving that the House should resolve itself into a committee to take into consideration the Lord-Lieutenant's message on the Wednesday following. On a division there appeared for the motion 158; and against it, 115. A majority consequently of forty-three were in favour of the Union.

This was the largest division ever known in the Irish Commons. Including the Speaker, two hundred and seventy-eight out of three hundred were present. Though some seats were vacant, and some members had paired, twenty-two only were absent.

Previous to the debate, Colonel Bagwell, on presenting a petition from the county of Tipperary against the Union, took occasion to say that, though he had supported the measure on the 15th of January preceding, he was now determined to oppose it. He grounded his change of action on the number and respectability of the names attached to the petition he had presented. This gentleman's desertion was attended by that of his two sons. Including the Bagwells, seven members of the Unionist party left the Government on this occasion, making a difference of fourteen votes on a division.

Two remarkable speeches were delivered in this debate. Mr. Dobbs, one of the members for Charlemont, had written a book to prove that a union with Great Britain was forbidden in the book of Daniel and the Revelation. On this occasion he concluded an able and high-minded speech with these words: "I tell you, sir, the hand of God has marked this country for His own. It was not for nothing that the harp of David with an angel in its front was made the arms of Ireland. It was not for nothing that the apostolic crown is the crown of Ireland. It was not for nothing that the serpent and every venomous creature has been banished from the land. I tell the noble Lord, I tell you, sir, and this House, and I proclaim it to the British and Irish nation, that the independence of Ireland is written in the immutable records of Heaven."[1]

The other was a speech of Richard Lovell Edgeworth, father of Maria Edgeworth. He commenced by saying that he had not made up his mind which way he should vote when he entered the House. He then proceeded to set forth the strongest arguments in favour of a Union, and ended with a violent philippic against the Government and the measure. "Notwithstanding," he added, "my own opinion is in favour of a Union."[2] On the 23rd of January in the preceding year this gentleman had also voted against the Government, stating at the same time that he thought the measure of Union advisable. Grattan delivered the second of his anti-Union orations in this debate.

In returning from the House to their respective homes some of the members were insulted by the populace for supporting the Union. The fear of personal injury induced an application to the Lord-Lieutenant for protection. At the next meeting of the House a guard of cavalry appeared for the preservation of peace and order. This measure of precaution was continued during the subsequent debates.

In the House of Lords on the 10th of February a motion was made to take into consideration the message relative to a Union. A debate followed, which was made remarkable by the memorable speech of Lord Clare. His speech lasted four hours, and produced an effect on

[1] *Report of Debate*, p. 179. Moore, Dublin, 1800.
[2] *Ib.* p. 207.

the Lords and on "the audience, which was uncommonly numerous,".[1] never surpassed by any delivered in a legislative assembly. It was in fact a review of the whole history of Ireland up to the moment of its delivery. Lords Downshire, Charlemont, and Bellamont spoke against the motion, but it was carried by a majority of forty-nine; the numbers being seventy-five for, and twenty-six against. The whole minority protested on this occasion.[2]

Lord Downshire in his speech condemned the conduct of the Irish Parliament at the time of the Regency dispute. He thought that that would have been the proper time for ministers to have introduced the question of union, and added that, if a period of tranquillity and peace were to arrive, and the subject were then brought forward and submitted to the consideration of the nation, he would give it his best assistance.

There were a few subsequent debates in the Upper House on some of the articles of Union, one particularly on the 22nd of March, when Chief Baron Yelverton made an able speech in favour of the measure. But, as its principle had been adopted by the Lords, and there was on every occasion a large majority for the Union, we shall not further refer to them.

On the 14th of February a motion was made in the

[1] *Corn. Corr.* iii. 184.
[2] Leinster, Downshire, Pery (by proxy), Meath, Granard, Ludlow (by proxy), Moira (by proxy), Arran, Charlemont, Kingston, Mountcashel, Farnham, Massy (by proxy), Enniskillen, Belmore (by proxy), Dillon, Strangford, Powerscourt, De Vesci (by proxy), William Down and Connor, Richard Waterford and Lismore, Louth, Lismore Sunderlin, Bellamont, Blaney.

House of Commons that a general Committee should proceed to the consideration of the terms of union. After the delivery of several speeches, a postponement was proposed by the Opposition with a view to the production of documents. This was rejected by a majority of thirty-seven. Another debate and a new division followed, when a hundred and fifty-seven to a hundred and ten refused to delay the discussion. Lord Castlereagh, having attained his object, which was to show that the Government majority was increasing, and that no impression had been made on the House since the last debate, consented to an adjournment.[1]

On the 17th, the day to which the House was adjourned, the resolution preliminary to the articles of Union was, after a debate of eighteen hours, carried by a majority of forty-six, the voting being 161 to 115. This resolution was: "That in order to promote and secure the essential interests of Great Britain and Ireland, and to consolidate the strength, power, and resources of the British Empire, it will be advisable to concur in such measures as may best tend to unite the two kingdoms in such manner and on such terms and conditions as may be established by Acts of the respective Parliaments of Great Britain and Ireland." In and by this resolution the principle of a Union was adopted. All that followed was merely the settlement of the precise conditions on which the incorporation should take place.

This was a stormy debate. In opening it the Chancellor of the Exchequer, Corry, adverted to the

[1] Lord Castlereagh at first suspected that the motion for adjournment was the result of a wish to delay the discussion.

inflammatory proceedings of men of education and property, and particularly to the speeches and writings of members of Parliament. He alluded specially to Grattan, and quoted many passages from his address to the citizens of Dublin, which he conceived had contributed to the late rebellion. Grattan vindicated himself in strong terms, whereupon Corry replied with increased severity. Grattan rejoined with greater warmth, "prodigally using terms of pointed censure and gross contumely, if not of scurrilous abuse."[1] Grattan's language produced a challenge from Corry. The hostile orators met in a duel, in which Corry was wounded, though not dangerously, as he was able to reappear in the House on the 19th.

Mr. William Johnson, afterwards a judge, in this debate indignantly denied the insinuations of corrupt influence thrown out against those who were in favour of a Union. "It was said," he exclaimed, "that they had been *bought*. But what had bought them? the state of the country and the fate of Europe. What had bought others had also bought him. The question had been forced upon him by the prevailing calamities, and he had examined it from no other motive or impulse than an anxious desire of meeting the peculiar evils of the country, which he reviewed under three aspects, constitution, internal quiet, and commerce."

On the 21st February, the first three articles of the plan of Union were carried without a division, and the first of the following January was fixed for the commencement of the Union.

[1] Coote's *Hist. of the Union*, 426.

On the 4th of March, George Ponsonby brought forward a motion respecting the sense of the nation on the subject of the Union. He said that His Majesty would not have persevered in recommending the measure unless he believed that the people were in its favour, and urged the House to remove this delusion by an intimation of the truth. A knowledge of the number of petitions against it would correct the error. He therefore proposed an address to the King, stating that petitions against the Union had been presented from twenty-six counties and various cities and towns. Lord Castlereagh replied that seventy-four declarations had been made in its favour by public bodies in the kingdom; that nineteen of these had proceeded from the freeholders of counties, and many of the remainder from the chief towns and cities. He contended that in these the true expression of the sense of the loyal and propertied classes was to be found. A general debate followed, which lasted till six o'clock in the morning, when the house divided on the question of adjournment, 155 for; 107 against—a majority for Government of forty-eight.

The discussion was renewed on the 13th of March, when Sir John Parnell moved that an address should be presented to the King, praying him to call a new Parliament before any final arrangement of a Union should be adopted. On this occasion, Mr. Saurin, a nominee of Lord Downshire, urged the expediency of attending to the sense of the nation, and maintained that, if laws should be enacted against the will of the public, they would not be obligatory, and the right of resistance would revert to the people. This doctrine was so dangerous that even Grattan felt it went too far, and he was obliged to soften it down by recommending the appeal not as a reference to the mere multitude, but to the constituent body only. Lord Castlereagh said the Parliament enjoyed the confidence both of His Majesty and the people, and that a dissolution was therefore unnecessary. He warmly repelled Saurin's doctrine as highly unconstitutional, and tending to sedition. The motion was negatived by a majority of forty-six.

When it was proposed on the 19th that the House should be resumed for the purpose of receiving the report of the committee, a debate took place. Grattan delivered his third oration against the Union on this occasion. Two divisions unfavourable to the Opposition took place; in one, Government had a majority of forty-two; in the other a majority of forty-seven.

The report being presented to the House on the 21st, the Opposition did not venture to challenge a division, as they thought it imprudent to risk another after the unfavourable results of the 19th. A meeting of the body had been held on the preceding day at Lord Charlemont's, when it was determined that there should be no contest on this occasion, but that the minor speakers of the party might, if they pleased, make protests against the measure. Accordingly, several of them, as Sir John Macartney, Mr. Burke, and Mr. Egan, delivered inflammatory speeches. After these gentlemen had expressed their sentiments, the resolutions received the sanction of the House. A message was then sent to the Lords, importing that the Commons had agreed to the articles of Union. On the 27th, the Peers intimated that they had adopted them with some alterations and additions. These amendments were readily approved by the Commons, and Lord Castlereagh immediately proposed an address, in which both Houses concurred. In it they declared that they cordially embraced the principle of incorporating Great Britain and Ireland into one kingdom by a complete and entire union of their legislatures. That they considered the resolutions of the British Parliament as wisely calculated to form the basis of such a settlement. That by these propositions they had been guided in their proceedings, and that the resolutions now offered by them were those articles which, if approved by the Parliament of Great Britain, they were ready to confirm and ratify, in order that the same might be established for ever by the mutual consent of both Parliaments.

The resolutions of the Irish Parliament were forwarded to England, and, being thence sent back, were referred by the Commons to a committee. A report was soon presented and examined. All the alterations in this were adopted by the Commons, and afterwards by the Peers.

On the 21st of May Lord Castlereagh moved for leave to bring in a Bill for the Union of Great Britain and Ireland. On this motion a debate took place, but the House was evidently tired of the subject, and unwilling to enter upon a fresh discussion. The House divided, and the motion was carried by a majority of sixty, the largest which had yet occurred.

On the 26th, after the Bill had been read a second

time, Grattan opposed its committal. He proposed a delay to the 1st of August, that it might be more fully examined. He again discussed the principle of the measure. It was a breach of a solemn covenant, on whose basis the separate, reciprocal, and conjoint power of the countries relied; an innovation promoted by the influence of martial law; an unauthorised assumption of a competency to destroy the independence of the realm, an unjustifiable attempt to injure the prosperity of the country. The Bill would be, *quoad* the Constitution, equivalent to a murder, and *quoad* the Government, a separation; and Ireland, by a Union, would be reduced to a state of slavery. This was the fourth and last of his anti-Union orations.

Lord Castlereagh censured Grattan for inviting future rebellion by cloaking it with the idea of liberty, and he asked whether it was the part of a good citizen to excite the people against a new system which was about to be established by the law of the land. The House divided early on the question of committal, which was carried by a majority of forty-five.

Grattan then rose and moved that the Bill should be committed on the 1st of September. He took this opportunity of making a personal attack on Lord Castlereagh. He made general charges of puerility, arrogance, and presumption. Lord Castlereagh replied with great calmness and dignity, and said he despised the idle parade of parliamentary spirit, which led to nothing, and which denied in offensive terms what had never been uttered. As a reasoner and debater, Lord Castlereagh was far superior to Grattan, and his conduct throughout this debate raised him greatly in the estimation of the House. An impartial witness who was present, Sir J. Crawford, was of opinion that "Lord Castlereagh had fairly thrown Grattan on his back."[1] A second division took place, when Grattan's motion was rejected by a majority of forty. A debate then followed on Lord Castlereagh's motion for committing the Bill for the ensuing Friday, which lasted till eleven o'clock. By this time the supporters of the Union, who had not expected an early division, were present, and when the question was put the Opposition declined to divide.

On the 6th of June Lord Corry moved that an address should be presented to the King praying that he would put an end to the measure of Union. The address was, in fact, a pamphlet, and is said by his son to have been drawn up by Grattan,[2] while Lord Cornwallis asserts that " it had been preparing for many days by a committee of the leaders of the Opposition ; " and adds, " I am informed the groundwork was laid by the Speaker." It occupies more than fourteen quarto pages of the appendix to Plowden's history, and took fifty minutes to read in the House. Grattan did not speak on this occasion. The motion for the address was rejected by a majority of fifty-eight. The report on the Union Bill was then received, and, upon the question that it should be read, the House again divided, and the reading was carried by a majority of sixty-five.

The Bill was read a third time on the 7th of June. In the debate which followed, and which was the last

[1] *Corn. Corr.* iii. 243. [2] *Grattan's Life,* v. app. 574.

on the Union, some violent speeches were delivered. Plunket talked of "the villany of Government." With the exception of Plunket, none of the greater actors took part in the discussion. Mr. Dobbs made an extraordinary harangue. He repeated his arguments against the Union, founded on the Book of Daniel and the Revelation. He declared his confident expectation of the speedy appearance of the Messiah as a temporal prince at Armagh. Entertaining these ideas, he was not alarmed at the progress of a Bill which he detested, as he was convinced it never would be operative.

After the Bill was read a third time in the Commons, it was carried up to the Peers by Lord Castlereagh. On its second reading in the Upper House Lords Farnham and Bellamont proposed some clauses which were negatived. It was then committed. It passed the committee without amendment, was reported in due form, and after an uninteresting debate, was read a third time and passed on the 13th of June by a majority of twenty-seven, the voting being forty-one to fourteen. The Royal assent was given on the 1st of August, the anniversary of the accession of the House of Brunswick to the British crown. The next day the Lord-Lieutenant put an end to the session with a Speech from the Throne.

CHAPTER VIII.

Accusations against the Government.—Compensation to the proprietors of boroughs.—Bestowal of peerages.—Alleged interference with the right of petitioning.—Dismissal of Government officials.

"PARLIAMENTARY reform," said Pitt in 1785, on introducing his scheme in the British House of Commons, " could only be brought about by two means, by an act of power, or by an adequate consideration which might induce bodies or individuals to part with rights which they considered as a species of valuable inheritance or of personal property. To a reform by violence he, and he was sensible many others, had an insurmountable objection, but he considered a reform in the representation of the people an object of such value and importance that he did not hesitate in his own mind to propose and to recommend to the House the establishment of a fund for the purpose of purchasing the franchise of such boroughs as might be induced to accept it under the circumstances which he had mentioned."[1] Pitt's proposal was to raise the sum of one million to purchase from thirty-six boroughs their right of returning members, and to distribute the seats

[1] Cobbett, *Parl. Hist.* xxv. 442.

thus acquired among the counties and populous towns. The sum proposed to be raised for the purchase of seats would have provided upwards of 27,000*l.* for each borough. But Pitt thought that this price was likely to be considered inadequate, for his plan further provided that, if any of the boroughs considered his offer insufficient, the money should go on accumulating until it reached an amount which would enable the Government to propose such terms as could not be refused. This scheme of Pitt's was approved and supported by, amongst many others, the high-minded Wilberforce.

Fifteen years afterwards, at the time of the Union, Pitt did not hesitate to offer to the proprietors of Irish boroughs terms of compensation for the loss of their rights, but their compensation was settled upon a much lower scale than that proposed for English proprietors. The Irish scheme was regulated by the then market value of such property, which was about 16,000*l.* for a borough and 8,000*l.* for a half borough, as all the Irish places returned two representatives. In 1797 the price of a borough was, as Grattan informs us, from 14,000*l.* to 16,000*l.*, and their value was rapidly rising.[1]

The growth of a private interest in Parliament and the practice of buying and selling the privilege of legislation were undoubtedly repugnant to the spirit and theory of representative government. But the ownership of boroughs had grown up insensibly, and they had long been looked upon and treated as private property.

[1] "It is known that the price of boroughs is from 14,000*l.* to 16,000*l.*, and has in the course of not many years increased one-third."—Address to the citizens of Dublin, 1797.

It has always been a characteristic of the English mind to pay regard to vested rights, if these rights have acquired strength from the custom of generations and the tacit acquiescence of the public. The dispensation of justice in a country affects all the subjects, and can never be regarded as the source of private advantage, yet when the heritable jurisdictions in Scotland were abolished, full compensation was granted to the individuals whose interests were affected.[1] In the case of the Irish boroughs it must be remembered that, as Grattan tells us, many of these had been originally granted by the crown to individuals as private property distinctly.[2] It is easy to see how the system of granting some boroughs to individuals as private possessions begot the idea that others might be legally acquired. We have seen that Grattan himself, who declaimed so often against borough ownership, purchased seats on two occasions. This custom was as general in England as in Ireland, and it did not excite any feeling of repugnance in that kingdom at this time. Many English statesmen believed that the system of private nomination to seats in Parliament was a good one, and pointed, as an argument in its favour, to its results. History informs us of a long line of distinguished men who owed to this custom their first introduction into public life. The names of many such will at once recur to our readers. We need only mention

[1] A sum of 161,000*l*. was paid on the abolition of these jurisdictions.

[2] "Most of the forty boroughs created by James were so. It appears from the grants themselves that they were intended to be private property."—*Parl. Reg.* xiii. 160.

some of these names : the great Lord Chatham, Pitt, Burke, Canning, Fox, Wyndham, Brougham, Sir Samuel Romilly, Lord North, Lord Granville, and the Marquis Wellesley in England; and Flood, Grattan and Plunket in Ireland. The system may have been bad in Ireland, but it was quite as bad in England, and infinitely worse in Scotland. In England 371 members out of 513 were nominated by the Government, by peers, and commoners. In Scotland there was not a single free seat, the whole of the Scotch members, forty-five in number, being nominated by peers or influential commoners.[1]

It has been objected that no compensation whatever should have been allowed to the proprietors of Irish boroughs, inasmuch as the return of members to Parliament is a public trust. It is hard to understand this squeamish delicacy of feeling in a generation which has witnessed the disestablishment of the Irish Church, and the payment of large sums to owners of livings for the withdrawal of their rights of patronage. The cases are exactly similar. If the return of members to Parliament is a public trust, the nomination of religious pastors is no less a sacred duty. If the patrons of livings may be compensated, surely the proprietors of boroughs deserved something to re-imburse them for the loss of long acknowledged rights, caused by a radical change in the constitution. But this nice criticism dis-

---

[1] In England and Wales the nominees of Government were sixteen; of peers, 218; of commoners, 137. In Scotland peers disposed of thirty-one seats; commoners of fourteen.—Oldfield's *Hist. of Representation*, vol. vi. 300.

regards the identity of the cases. It is wrong, exclaims this narrow and peevish morality, to buy the power of returning members to an earthly Parliament; it is right to purchase the power of nominating the ministers of God.

To have refused compensation to the owners of boroughs in Ireland would have had the effect of virtually packing the House of Lords against the Union, for men could not have been expected to vote for a measure which they knew would deprive them of a valuable property. It would have stirred up the proprietors of these places as a body to use whatever influence they possessed over the representatives of the people for the purpose of biassing their judgment and defeating the measure. The only way to render them impartial and capable of weighing coolly the advantages and disadvantages of the Union, was to offer a fair and reasonable compensation for the loss of rights which had grown up by the tacit endurance of the Government and of the people.

The Act[1] for making compensation to bodies corporate and individuals in respect of such places as should cease to return members after the Union, was, if not drawn in England, seen and examined by Pitt, who advised that its terms should be liberal.[2] It was introduced into the Irish Commons in June, 1800,

---

[1] 40 George III. c. 34.

[2] "I inclose the draft of the Compensation Bill, which your lordship may put into the way of being completed. Upon your queries, Mr. Pitt wishes the liberal line to be adopted."—Cooke to Lord Castlereagh, *Cast. Corr.* iii. 300.

and was read a third time within the same month. During its progress through the Lower House it never met with an opposition numbering more than seven. In the Lords one member dissented and three protested against it. But their protest was not grounded on any accusation of corruption; indeed, one of the peers who protested — Lord Belmore — received 30,000*l*. for his two boroughs of Ballyshannon and Belturbet.

The Act established a Court for the proof of losses, and provided that sworn Commissioners should ascertain, on the oaths of informants, what allowances and compensation should be given to bodies corporate and individuals in respect of towns and boroughs which should cease to return members. A sum of 15,000*l*. was to be awarded for each place ceasing to send any representative, and payment of the compensation was to be made by five annual instalments of twenty per cent. each. There was no concealment whatever; the Court and the Act establishing it were equally public. The provision was general and not one-sided, and we shall see that the anti-Unionists took full advantage of it, in the proportion of their numbers when compared with that of the Unionists. If the compensation given by this Court and under this public Act amounted to bribery, the English and Irish noblemen and gentlemen who availed themselves of the opportunity were content to receive the wages of corruption openly and in the light of day.

The Act was limited to places which should cease to return *any* member. If the place was completely disfranchised, the sum of 15,000*l.* was to be paid to its proprietors, or to the borough itself. If, on the other hand, the place continued to send a member, a single seat in the Imperial Parliament was to be considered as of equal value with the two former seats in the Irish legislature, and no compensation whatever in money was to be given in this case.

Eighty-four boroughs were completely disfranchised by the Act of Union, and thirty-four places were retained as returning members to the united Parliament. The places retained were to return each one member, with the exception of Dublin and Cork, which were allowed two respectively.

As eighty-four places were disfranchised, there was a sum of 1,260,000*l.* paid under the Act. As it has been, and still is, alleged, that the Act of Union was carried by this system of compensation to the proprietors of Irish boroughs—or bribery, as it is called —it becomes necessary to examine the question.

Let us see how much of this sum was paid to persons who could have used their influence in passing the Act, or to those who voted for that measure. There are certain amounts which must be deducted from the principal sum before we can estimate the moneys which were distributed among those Irish proprietors who were likely to exercise any influence direct or indirect on those who voted in the House of Commons for the Union.

1. A sum of 67,500*l.* was paid to Englishmen who owned boroughs in Ireland. Of this amount, the Duke of Devonshire received 30,000*l.*; Lord Darnley,

15,000*l.* ; Lord Wellesley,[1] 15,000*l.* ; and Lord Lyttelton, 7,500*l.*[2] Here it may be remarked that if the Irish proprietors were bribed by the compensation paid to them for their boroughs, these Englishmen were also bribed. To what absurdities are we driven by this accusation ! The Duke of Devonshire, one of our greatest English nobles, and the head of a historic house, bribed : and that not secretly, but openly and under a public Act of Parliament ! The intelligence of that man is not to be envied who can believe that such a thing is even possible.

2. A sum of 60,000*l.* was awarded to the four boroughs which had no owners. These boroughs were St. Canice, Clogher, Old Leighlin and Swords. The compensation for the first three was paid to the Commissioners of First Fruits, to be laid out and invested in the public funds, and the annual proceeds thereof to be applied to the same uses and purposes to which the first fruits were applicable by law, and in such a manner as should lead most effectually to promote the residence of the clergy. The compensation awarded to the borough of Swords was paid to the Lord Chancellor, the Archbishop of Dublin and others, as trustees, to be laid out by them in building schools and in other works for the general use of the town.[3]

3. A sum of 30,000*l.* was paid to the executors of Henry Bruen, who died in 1795, before the Union was

---

[1] Lord Wellesley is called an Englishman, as his whole career was English.
[2] *Liber Munerum Pub. Hiberniæ*, part vii. 171.
[3] *Ib.*

even talked of,[1] and 18,750*l.* was paid to two ladies—the Countess of Wicklow and the Countess of Lanesborough.[2]

If we deduct these amounts from the principal sum, there will remain a sum of about 1,100,000*l.*, which was distributed among Irishmen who were the proprietors of boroughs or shares in them. Now, of this amount, upwards of 400,000*l.* was actually paid to anti-Unionists.[3] The question arises—were these men bribed? Members of both Houses who had opposed the Union by every means in their power, even Peers who protested against the measure, and whose protests may still be read in their journals, felt no shame in receiving the allowance given by law for their boroughs, for they considered it not as a bribe, but as fair compensation.

The cases of some of the leading anti-Unionists in the Lords and Commons, may be mentioned here.

The Duke of Leinster during the whole progress of the Union opposed it, and protested against it, yet he received 28,800*l.* as compensation; 15,000*l.* for the borough of Kildare, and 13,800*l.* for his share in that of Athy.

The whole of Lord Downshire's enormous influence[4]

---

[1] As to the date of his death see *Corn. Corr.* i. 157.

[2] *Liber Munerum Pub. Hiberniæ*, part vii. 171.

[3] The sum given to anti-Unionists was 434,850*l.*

[4] " Down county contains 30,000 freeholders, who elect the friends of the Marquis of Downshire without contest. To insure this object, the Marquis's estate has been divided, sub-divided, and again divided until it has become a *warren* of freeholders, and the scheme has completely succeeded."—Wakefield's *Ireland*, ii. 304.

was directed against the Union. He was able to obtain the signatures of 17,500 freeholders of his county to a petition against the Union in 1800. He even overpassed, as we have seen, the limits of legality in his opposition to it, yet he received 52,000*l.* for his boroughs and shares of boroughs.

Lord Granard protested against the Union; yet he obtained 30,000*l.* for his boroughs of Mullingar and St. Johnstown.

Lord Belmore protested, and his son, Lord Corry, was, as we have seen, a leading and influential anti-Unionist in the Commons. Lord Belmore received 30,000*l.* for his boroughs of Ballyshannon and Belturbet.

Lord Lismore protested. This nobleman was paid 22,500*l.*; 15,000*l.* for the borough of Enniscorthy, and 7,500*l.* for a share in Fethard.

Lords Charlemont, Kingstown, and Arran protested; yet they received 15,000*l.* each, for their boroughs of Charlemont, Boyle, and Donegal.

Lords Ludlow and Belvedere protested. The former received 7,500*l.*, the latter 3,750*l.*, for their shares in boroughs.

We see the same readiness to avail themselves of the Act allowing compensation in the leaders of the anti-Unionists in the House of Commons.

The Speaker, the Right Honourable John Foster, the recognised leader of the anti-Unionists, received 7,500*l.* for a half-share in the borough of Dunleer.[1]

[1] This gentleman also received an annuity of 5,038*l.* 8*s.* 4*d.* as compensation for his office of Speaker.

The Right Honourable George Ponsonby, afterwards Lord Chancellor of Ireland, and for some years the leader of the Opposition in the British House of Commons, the friend of Grattan, and the sharer in all his views of reform, received 15,000*l.* for his borough of Banagher.

Sir John Parnell, second only to Mr. Foster in the ranks of the anti-Unionists, received 7,500*l.* for his half share in Maryborough.

Mr. Tighe, a steady and honourable opponent of the measure, received 30,000*l.* for his two boroughs of Inistiogue and Wicklow.

Sir John Freke, John Latouche, Gustavus Lambart, the Buxton family, and that of the Kings, accepted each 15,000*l.*, and Henry Coddington 7,500*l.*

There was not a single borough proprietor, whether English or Irish, who did not accept the compensation offered to him under the Act. In 1783 several of the Irish proprietors voluntarily proposed to give up their rights of private nomination without any remuneration whatever, in order to help forward a scheme of reform.[1] Yet the whole body of these proprietors, without an exception, in 1800 accepted the terms offered to them. How is it to be accounted for that there was not one high-minded man among them in this latter year, except on the supposition that all felt they could receive with a clear conscience a compensation for their rights and privileges ?

In fact, the Act did not provide compensation of any kind for many of these proprietors. The rule, that all

[1] *History of the Proceedings and Debates of the Volunteers, Dublin,* 1784.

places should be excluded from allowances from which members were to be sent to the Imperial Parliament, and that one seat in it should be considered as of equal value with two seats in the Irish House, was rigidly carried out, and the effect of the rule was to deprive many patrons of any compensation at all. Thus, Lord De Clifford was able to return four members,[1] two from Kinsale and two from Downpatrick; but, as these boroughs retained one seat each, no compensation was allowed. Lord Ely for a seat at Wexford; Lord Shannon, for a seat at Youghal; the Duke of Devonshire for one at Bandon, and one at Dungarvan; and Lord Abercorn for two at Dungannon received no compensation. The Primate could return two members at Armagh, yet no allowance was made to him. The patrons of Belfast, Carlow, New Ross, Ennis, Tralee, and Sligo, within which places the voters numbered only thirteen, and where the elections were entirely under the control of individuals, were allowed no compensation. The same was the case, with the difference of a small increase in the number of electors, at Athlone, Cashel, Clonmel, Coleraine, Dundalk, Enniskillen, Lisburn, and Portarlington, yet no compensation was given to the persons who decided the returns at these places.[2] It is absurd to say that the terms allowed under the Act compensated the owners of Irish boroughs, as a body,

[1] *Corn. Corr.* iii. 43.
[2] See *Corn. Corr.* iii. 234, where it is stated, "a contest had scarcely ever occurred in any of them." In Portarlington and Enniskillen the number of electors was fifteen; in Cashel twenty-six; in Dundalk thirty-two; in Coleraine thirty-six; in Lisburn fifty-six; in Clonmel 105; in Athlone seventy-one.

for the rights and privileges which the Union took away.

Even those proprietors who were paid at the rate of 15,000*l*. for a borough, or 7,500*l*. for a half, were barely compensated, if compensation means a full equivalent for property taken away. In 1793, Grattan informs us,[1] the price of a seat had risen to 3,000*l*., and Lord Castlereagh in 1799 estimated it at 4000*l*.[2] The Parliament lasted for eight years. This sum of 3,000*l*. for a seat would allow the owner about 5 per cent. for the money expended on the purchase, and besides he had many chances in his favour. The death or promotion of the sitting member, his removal—if a military man—to a foreign station, or a dissolution of Parliament, restored the seat to its proprietor, who might sell it anew. If we add to these considerations the prestige such property afforded to its owner, we can hardly estimate 15,000*l*. for a borough carrying with it the perpetual right of nominating two members, or 7,500*l*. for its half, a full compensation, particularly when it is remembered that the payment was not concluded till the expiration of five years.

But if we look closer at the matter, is not this idea of bribing the borough proprietors and passing the Act of Union by their influence, far fetched and a little unintelligible? What had these proprietors to do with the passing of the Act through the Commons? They were merely reversioners, and the decision of the question rested not with them, but with their tenants in possession. To bribe the three hundred members of the

[1] *Parl. Reg.* xiii. 162. [2] *Cast. Corr.* ii. 150.

House of Commons would surpass the means of any Government. Yet, this is the body which the Government, if they had any idea of bribery, would have naturally approached. The last Irish Parliament which accepted the Union met on the 9th of January, 1798, and in 1800 there were still five years of its life to run. During this time the borough proprietors had no authority to interfere with the judgment or decision of its members. A large number of these had purchased their seats, and were perfectly independent of the patrons.[1] They would certainly have resented any attempt to coerce their opinion, particularly on such a question as the continuance of the assembly in which they sat. No doubt some members had been returned by the patrons from motives of confidence or affection, but even these nominees could not have been expected to yield on such a momentous occasion, and to sacrifice all their future hopes of distinction and advancement. How are we to account for the blindness of Government in attempting to allure with their bribes the intermediate borough proprietors, who had only at the best a very indirect influence, and neglecting the real and efficient factors? We shall leave the question to be answered by those who declaim without proof against the corruption of the English Government.

In opposition to declamation and the insinuation of the bribery of individual members we have positive evidence. Lord Castlereagh, Lord Hawkesley, Sir John

[1] There were fifty barristers in the last Irish Parliament. Lord Castlereagh thought that they gave 4,000*l.* each for their seats.— *Cast. Corr.* ii. 151.

Blaquiere, the Prime Serjeant, and Chancellor Corry in their places in Parliament always met with a direct denial this charge of corruption; and when the allegations were challenged, the accusers did not venture to bring forward their proofs.[1] Though the opponents of the Union attempted unsuccessfully to substantiate their accusation of intimidation, they never made an effort to prove any case of bribery. On the 8th of February, 1800, a late period in the contest, Lord Cornwallis in a private letter to his brother, writes in such a manner as shows that the Government neither had the means to bribe, nor the wish to resort to such proceedings: "The enemy to my certain knowledge, offer 5,000*l*. ready money for a vote; *if we had the means* and were disposed to make such vile use of them, we dare not trust the credit of Government in the hands of such rascals."[2] Lord Plunket was one of those who, in the heat of the Union debates, most frequently made the charge of corruption[3] against the English Government. In 1803, Plunket was appointed Solicitor-General, and on the death of Lord Castlereagh he wrote in 1823 to that nobleman's brother a letter of condolence, in which he thus speaks of the deceased statesman: "Your lordship does me no more than justice in estimating the feelings with which the memory of the late Marquis of Londonderry affects and must ever affect my mind. His friendship and confidence were the prime causes which induced His Majesty's Government to desire my services. And I can truly add that my unreserved reliance on the cordiality of his

---

[1] See next chapter.   [2] *Corn. Corr.* iii. 184.
[3] "The black corruption of the Castle," as he termed it.

feelings towards me, joined to my perfect knowledge of the wisdom and liberality of all his public objects and opinions, were the principal causes which induced me to accept the honour which was proposed to me. Nothing can ever occur to me in political life so calamitous as the event which, in common with all his country and Europe, I deeply deplore."

Are these the words of a man who believed that Lord Castlereagh carried the Union by a mixture of intrigue and violence? Plunket was the most formidable and most eloquent of the opponents of that measure, and never relaxed in his efforts against it. His subsequent career, and the splendour of his advocacy of the Catholic claims are well known. Is it possible to come to the conclusion that, if he had believed the accusations of corruption, he would have accepted office under Lord Castlereagh at a time when the Union proceedings were still fresh in his mind, and that after many years he would have attended his obsequies with praise of "all his public objects and opinions"?

Another accusation has been brought against Pitt and the English Government—that by a lavish bestowal of peerages they bribed or corrupted the Irish Parliament. It is misleading to speak of the "Irish Government" in this matter as is sometimes done, for there has never been in Ireland such a thing since the time of James II. The Irish Chief Governor is the minister and servant of the Central Executive, with which he is in constant communication, and the orders and policy of which he merely carries out. This accusation has only to be fairly looked at to vanish into thin air. The

o

only wonder is that at least twice the number of peerages was not granted. In 1779, Lord North in one day, and on no special occasion, created eighteen Irish peerages, and raised five viscounts and seven barons a step in their order; that is thirty in all.[1] In 1800, after a protracted contest which lasted nearly two years—after a fundamental change in the Irish peerage, which, from a self-representative became a represented body—after services which statesmen seldom obtain from their supporters, and which, if the Union had not been carried, would certainly have excluded those followers from public life for the remainder of their days—and after the Unionists had borne every contumely and reproach during the long struggle, for the anti-Unionists represented their opponents as venal traitors to their country —Pitt rewarded forty[2] of his followers. With a sparing hand he created twenty new Irish peerages; sixteen peers were promoted a step in their order, and four English peerages were granted.[3] The vast majority

---

[1] Lecky, iv. 441.

[2] In the list of Union honours given by the editor of the *Cornwallis Correspondence*, there are at least six mistakes. Lord Inchiquin obtained neither his Irish marquisate nor his English barony for Union services. "Lord Inchiquin," says Cornwallis, "has not the smallest weight or consequence in this country." The Bandon and O'Neill peerages had been promised before the rebellion broke out (*Corn. Corr.* iii. 245). Lord Henniker did not obtain his peerage for such services (*ib.* iii. 246); nor did Lord Erris. Lord Cornwallis, though he transmitted Colonel King's request for this honour, refused to recommend it (*ib.* iii. 311). It is extremely doubtful whether Lord Charles Fitzgerald received his Barony of Lecale, or Viscount Castlestewart his earldom, for any such services.

[3] Five Irish peers were created to the English peerage, but one of

who had borne the heat of the day, and who had contributed no small share to the extinction of the rebellion, were dismissed without a word of commendation or a mark of regard.[1]

At the end of every session of Parliament we are astonished to hear of the elevation of many to the peerage who are not a whit taller or better than their fellow-men, and whose only claim to such an honour is that they have supported their party. Yet we affect to wonder at the comparatively few creations which marked the end of a lengthened and momentous contest that divided families and excited an amount of bitterness rarely to be found in political struggles. In the conflict respecting the Union, the Government had to oppose an aristocratic and powerful faction, and during its whole progress their supporters were exposed to rancorous imputations and party hatred. Pitt did well to recompense some of the followers who throughout this long struggle never failed him, and never relaxed their assistance in passing a measure which they believed to be essential to the salvation of their country. But he did ill in forgetting the eminent services which the Irish peerage and gentry had rendered in putting down the rebellion. If we further consider that the removal of

these was Lord Inchiquin, who did not receive his peerage for Union services.—*Corn. Corr.* iii. 264.

[1] "Our friends have submitted to the severest attendance ever known in the history of Parliament with unexampled patience.... Our sittings have never broken up earlier than twelve at night, and have frequently lasted till twelve in the day. Many of our friends are really confined on account of illness contracted by attendance." —*Ib.* iii. 206.

the Irish Parliament to Westminster, and the diminution of the number of Irish lords and representatives in the united Parliament, lessened the importance and position of those who were thus excluded from public life ;[1] and that the Government ought to have shown every intention to conciliate Irish feeling, and met with a liberal response every claim which might be advanced, we can only wonder that these honours were not distributed with a more liberal hand.[2]

We have said that five British peerages were granted to Irish peers, four of them to Pitt's supporters. The number should have been much greater. This abstemious creation was owing to feelings of jealousy in the English aristocracy. One of the objections made to the Union by its opponents was that Ireland would not be sufficiently represented in the Imperial House of Lords. There were then about 320 members in that assembly. By the Act of Union twenty-eight representative peers and four ecclesiastical dignitaries only were to be sent from Ireland. The number of Irish peers who also had seats in the British House was very small. If, instead of five, twenty English peerages had been distributed among the Irish aristocracy, no reasonable man could have complained, for they well deserved such a return for their conduct in the extinction of the rebellion. Yet if such a scheme had been adopted, what a weight it would have lent to the baseless declamation against the Union.

[1] "This measure [the Union] goes to new-model the public consequence of every man in Parliament, and to diminish most materially the authority of the most powerful."—*Corn. Corr.* iii. 122.

[2] See Lord Brabourne's *Facts and Fictions of Irish History*, 1886, where this last consideration is fully and forcibly urged.

A freer hand, a larger discretion is allowed to ministers in England, but every step of the Government in Ireland is dogged with suspicion and followed by complaints or accusations. All the ideas of Irishmen respecting constitutional administration are necessarily derived from the practice of England. It may therefore be instructive to mention some of the peerage creations which have taken place in that country. In 1711, twelve peers were created in a batch to turn a majority in favour of the Court, which they did on the very day of their introduction.[1] In 1776, on a question respecting the Civil list, ten new peers were made, three were promoted to earldoms, and one raised to the dignity of viscount. Within the space of two years, in 1796 to 1797, about the same period as the Union contest lasted in Ireland, thirty-five peers were created or promoted.[2] At the time of the Reform Bill, not a more important measure than that of the Union, Lord Grey contemplated the creation of nearly 100 peers[3] for the purpose of securing a majority. "When I went to Windsor with Lord Grey," says Brougham, "I had a list of eighty creations, framed upon the principle of making the least possible permanent addition to our House and to the aristocracy by calling up peers' eldest sons, by choosing men without families, by taking Scotch and Irish peers." The King himself gave his permission in writing to Lord Grey to create an un-

---

[1] They were asked in derision whether they would vote individually or, like a jury, by their foreman.
[2] May, *Const. Hist.* i. 233.   [3] *Ib.* i. 236.

limited number.[1] Nor did the proposal excite any repugnance in the public mind. On the 7th of January, 1832, Sydney Smith wrote to Lady Grey that everybody expected such a creation as a matter of course, adding his own opinion: "I am for forty, to make things safe in committee." Many of Lord Grey's friends and all the Liberal press concurred in this advice.

The contest for Reform in 1832 and that for the Union in 1800 were similar in this respect. Both were struggles in which the Government, backed by the people, contended with a powerful aristocracy for privileges which had been long enjoyed without question, but which belonged to the public. In England the coercion of the House of Lords by the threat of an indefinite creation of peers has never been blamed. In Ireland the granting of a small number of peerages after a long period of service, and for the purpose of extinguishing what Lord Castlereagh well called "the fee simple of Irish corruption," has ever been declaimed against as bribery and baseness.

On two occasions only during the long discussion on the Union, did the anti-Unionists venture to put their accusations against the Government to the proof. On these occasions charges were brought that Government or its agents violated the liberties of the subjects by preventing them from meeting to petition Parliament against the Union. The first of these charges was made

---

[1] "The King grants permission to Earl Grey and to his Chancellor, Lord Brougham, to create such a number of peers as will be sufficient to assure the passing of the Reform Bill, first calling up peers' eldest sons.—WILLIAM R."

on the 9th February, 1799, when Mr., afterwards Sir Jonah Barrington, alleged that Sir Charles Asgill had prevented the mayor of Clonmel from holding a meeting to discuss the measure of Union by the interference of the military power, though a public request had been made to the mayor to call such a meeting.

This accusation was brought forward without any proof or documents to support it, and deservedly subjected its mover to the reproof of the Attorney-General for having challenged the conduct of a public officer without any evidence. The facts were, Sir Charles Asgill had learned that the mayor was about to summon a meeting to discuss the Union. The meeting was not confined to the town, but was to be general and indiscriminate. Sir Charles warned the mayor that such an assembly, not limited to his townsmen, would be extremely hazardous for the peace of the place so soon after the rebellion, and in a proclaimed district. He also stated that if the mayor insisted on calling the meeting, that officer must be answerable for the consequences, but that there was no objection of any kind to the mayor's calling a meeting of the freeholders and inhabitants of the town. Mr. Barrington attempted to justify his conduct, but the Speaker interfered, and the matter ended there.[1] It is evident that if there had been anything in the matter, the charge would have been pressed home. The anti-Unionists had a majority at this time in the House, and they were flushed with their recent victory over the Government on the 24th of January preceding. An accusation of this kind, if

[1] *Belfast News Letter*, 15th Feb. 1799.

successfully urged, would have seriously affected subsequent divisions.

The second occasion was on the 5th of February, 1800. Sir Lawrence Parsons, on that day, accused Major Rogers, the Commandant at Birr, and the high sheriff, Mr. Darby, of having attempted to prevent a meeting of the freeholders of Birr, on Sunday, the 2nd of February, which was called to petition against the Union, and of having threatened to disperse it by military force. The Opposition hoped to prove the accusation, and also that it was by the orders of Government that the attempt was made to prevent or intimidate the meeting.[1] The charge was investigated by the House of Commons. After a long examination of witnesses, it appeared that there was no attempt whatever made to prevent the meeting. That, on the contrary, the high sheriff, though he considered such a meeting on a Sunday illegal, allowed it, lest any advantage should be taken of his interference to inflame the people; and that the measures taken by Major Rogers had been taken on the express directions of the high sheriff, who had merely desired him to hold himself in readiness in case a tumult should arise. It further appeared that Major Rogers had received express orders from the Lord-Lieutenant not to interfere, but to allow the meeting to assemble without interruption.[2]

The House was unanimous as to the conduct of the persons accused, and only differed as to the degree of praise which should be awarded to them. At length,

[1] *Corn. Corr.* iii. 190.   [2] *Ib.*

Mr. Plunket moved an amendment to insert certain words in the vote of approbation. The amendment was carried, and the entire resolution as amended runs in these words : "That the conduct of Verney Darby, Esq., late high sheriff of the King's County, and the conduct of Major Rogers, have not been intended to interfere with the undoubted right of the people of Ireland to petition their representatives in Parliament, but have been solely directed with a view to the preservation of the public peace : that it has been loyal, expedient, and meritorious, and is altogether highly deserving the approbation of this House."[1]

During the long struggle of the Union, seven members only of the Opposition were dismissed by the Government from offices held during pleasure. These were Sir John Parnell, Chancellor of the Exchequer; James Fitzgerald, the Prime Sergeant; Colonel Foster, a son of the Speaker, and four inferior officers whose names are given below.[2] It was absolutely necessary to dismiss the Chancellor of the Exchequer and the Prime Sergeant, if the Government wished to show that they were in earnest in proposing the measure of a Union. The Chancellorship and the Prime Sergeantcy were two of the greatest offices in the country. The Chancellor of the Exchequer represented the Government in the House of Commons on all matters of trade

[1] *Journals of the House of Commons*, xix. pt. i. 41.

[2] Colonel Wolfe, Commissioner of Revenue; Mr. Neville, Commissioner of Accounts; Major C. Hamilton, Barrack Board ; Mr. H. Hamilton, Cursitor in Chancery. Mr. J. B. Beresford and the Hon. George Knox were not dismissed; they resigned.—*Corn. Corr.* iii. 45, 51.

and finance. The Prime Sergeant took precedence of the Attorney-General, and his position was the first and most lucrative in the profession of the law. The holders of these offices were the consulting advisers of the administration, and both were members of the Privy Council. It was their duty to propose and recommend to the House every measure which the Government in its wisdom thought right to bring forward. To have proceeded with the Union, and at the same time to have retained in office and employ two of the most determined opponents of the measure, would have been absurd and paradoxical. The only effect of such conduct would have been to implant in the mind of the public, doubts and suspicions of the sincerity of Government.

Colonel Foster was dismissed on the ground that he had voted against the Government, and that he was the son of the Speaker, the declared enemy of the Union. "In particular," writes Pitt on the 26th January, 1799, "it strikes me as essential not to make an exception to this line in the instance of the Speaker's son. No Government can stand on a safe and respectable ground which does not show that it feels itself independent of him. With respect to persons of less note, or those who have been only neutral, more lenity may perhaps be advisable."[1] To the same effect the Duke of Portland writes in the same month. "It may be necessary to make the Speaker himself and the country sensible that his rank and situation cannot preserve their employments

[1] *Corn. Corr.* iii. 57.

to such of his family and dependants as act in opposition to the measures of Government."[1]

With respect to the dismissal of the four other officers, students of the Cornwallis and Castlereagh correspondence know how unwilling the Government was to remove any of the minor officials.[2] But there are certain considerations to be kept in mind when we judge of the wisdom of these dismissals. We must, above all, remember the great difference which existed between a Government official in England and one in Ireland. In England, an unfavourable vote of the House of Commons overturned the ministry, and with the ministry, fell all those who held subordinate offices at pleasure. This liability to go out with the Government, determined the action and votes of its supporters, and kept them true to the party upon which they depended. But a change of ministry in England hardly affected such persons in Ireland. If they had attached themselves to a powerful parliamentary interest, they were too strong for the King's representative, nor could they be dismissed without alienating the party to which they belonged. The consequence of this state of things was, that the King's Irish servants had for many years shown themselves capricious and impracticable, veering and changing about, as they thought their own immediate interests required. They were little disposed to lend a steady and continued support to any Government. Now that Pitt was resolved to make the Union " the grand and primary object of all his policy towards

[1] *Cast. Corr.* ii. 136.
[2] *Corn. Corr.* iii. 46, 47. *Cast. Corr.* ii. 136.

Ireland,"[1] he determined to break down this system of selfish oscillation, and for that purpose to make use of the means the Constitution afforded him. Accordingly, at the very commencement of the struggle, in January, 1799, he dismissed a few, but only a few, of the recalcitrant Government officials. As the contest proceeded, and Pitt became assured of the change of feeling which had come over the country, his Government disdained to take any notice of those who voted against the measure.

It has been the invariable constitutional custom in England to dismiss those members of the Government or officials who, on any grave question of policy, oppose the ministry. For a slight act of insubordination Mr. Huskisson was summarily ejected from the administration in 1828. It was proposed at this time that the two members which the disfranchised borough of East Retford had lost should be given to Birmingham. The Premier, the Duke of Wellington, was of opinion that they should be given to the hundred in which East Retford was situated. Mr. Huskisson voted for the former proposition, and was at once dismissed. The answer of the Duke to the excuse that Huskisson probably acted under a mistake, is well known. "There is no mistake, and there must be no mistake in the matter." In 1831 reports of dissensions in the Cabinet on the question of the Reform Bill had got abroad. To give these reports an authoritative contradiction and to restore popular confidence in the sincerity of the administration, Lord Grey insisted on the dismissal of Lord Howe, the

[1] His own words, *Corn. Corr.* iii. 57.

Queen's Chamberlain, and other officers of Her Majesty's household, who in their own persons or those of their near relatives and connections had opposed the Bill. In 1839 the principle was carried even farther by Sir Robert Peel. This statesman refused to undertake the formation of a ministry unless the Queen would dismiss her bed-chamber women, and that merely because they were relatives of those who were opposed to his policy. If in England, in 1831 and 1839, even the friends and connections of the opponents of the ministry were rightly regarded as dangerous enemies, and if in the former year many such were dismissed for the purpose of gaining the confidence of the public in the Cabinet, how much more necessary was it in Ireland to remove refractory officials, who by their own votes opposed the measure introduced by Government. To establish a conviction in the popular mind in 1800, that the Government considered a Union of transcendent importance to both countries, and that it was their fixed intention to persevere with it, it was indispensable to get rid of such of their own officers as were hostile to the measure.

CHAPTER IX.

Accusations against the Government (*continued*). — Money payments to members for their votes.—Military terrorism.

IT has been often, and is still, alleged that money payments were made by the Government to Irish members for their votes. This accusation rests on extracts from a few letters of Lord Castlereagh contained in the Cornwallis correspondence. We shall lay before our readers the whole of the evidence, which appears to us defective as proof, and hardly sufficient to excite more than a passing doubt in the mind of an impartial man. There is really but one letter of Lord Castlereagh, dated the 27th of February, 1800, which can give rise to suspicion. When we come to examine the position of the Government at the time this letter was written, and for twelve months previously, and also all the circumstances which existed at that moment, our suspicion will be greatly modified, if not entirely removed.

If it were the case that this letter, which gives rise to our doubts, was written at a time when the Government was hard pressed, or even soon after the time of such pressure, we ought undoubtedly to start in this examination with a strong presumption *against* the Government.

For it would be expecting too much from them to believe that they would have hesitated at some expenditure, at a time when the opposition was resorting to open and undisguised bribery, and when they themselves were endeavouring to carry a measure which was ardently desired by the English people,[1] and which they considered to be necessary for the salvation of the country.[2] But such was very far from being the case. From the first suggestion of a Union, the Government had an overwhelming majority in the Lords. In the House of Commons, it is true that a small majority of five had, on the 24th of January, 1799, at the beginning of the contest and before that Assembly or the country had time for reflection, refused to entertain the measure. But on the very first occasion on which a clear issue was knit between the Government and their opponents, viz., on Lord Corry's motion on the 15th of February, 1799, for a committee on the state of the nation, there was a decided majority of twenty for the Government and this too only three weeks after the first mention of a Union. During the remainder of the Session of 1799, the growing strength of the Government, and the decline of the Opposition were clearly manifested. The Regency Bill, introduced by the anti-Unionists, was shattered to pieces by the unanswerable arguments of Lord Castlereagh, and finally dropped.[3] In the only other division on the

[1] The British House of Commons then consisted of 558 members. There never were more than thirty opponents of the Union among them.

[2] "This country could not be saved without the Union."— Cornwallis to Ross. *Corn. Corr.* iii. 249.

[3] "The clauses (in the Regency Bill) which had been struck out

question of Union in this year, viz., on the 15th of May, the Government was successful by a majority of fifteen in a thin house of seventy-nine. In other matters also during this session, the Government was equally successful. Thus in the two divisions on the Martial Law or Rebellion Act, which the anti-Unionists opposed with all their might, a motion to delay the committee for one day only, was negatived by seventy-two votes to thirty-three, and the sole amendment proposed was rejected by a hundred and twenty-one votes to eighteen.[1] This very large majority arose from the support of the country gentlemen who rallied round the Government.[2]

The Parliament rose on the 1st of June, 1799. We have seen how the country manifested its desire for a Union during the seven months which elapsed between the rising of Parliament and its re-assembling on the 16th of January, 1800. On the first division in the new year, which took place on the first day of the meeting of Parliament, the Government had a majority of forty-two on the Union question. On the 5th of February the majority on the same measure was forty-three. On the 18th of February it was forty-six. On the 4th of March it was forty-eight. On the 21st of May it rose to sixty, and finally to sixty-five on the 6th of June.

If we keep in mind the preponderance of the Government in the House of Commons from the 15th of February, 1799, throughout the rest of the Session, and

in committee were printed in the form of notes to the Bill, and were as much at variance with the clauses which had been let to stand as these latter were inconsistent among themselves."—Baron Smith, letter to Foster, the Speaker, 1799.

[1] *Corn. Corr.* iii. 62.   [2] *Ib.*

the enthusiasm the country manifested from the rising of Parliament on the 1st of June till its meeting again in January, 1800, it is impossible to deny that the Union was practically carried in 1799, and that in 1800 the Government had only to collect the fruits of its victory.

There are in the Cornwallis Correspondence many letters, which passed between the Government and their Irish servants, labelled "Secret and Confidential," "Private and Confidential," "Most Secret and Confidential." Yet with the exception of the few letters of Lord Castlereagh, on which this accusation is based, there is not a word which can excite a shadow of suspicion that money payments were made to Irish members. Even in those letters from Ireland which complain that an Opposition Fund was established for the purpose of bribery, there is no hint or allusion which can be tortured into a suggestion that the Irish ministers ever entertained an idea of fighting with similar weapons. On the contrary, we have the declaration of Lord Cornwallis that he had not the means to bribe, and that if he had, he could not venture to risk the credit of Government in the hands "of such rascals" as would accept the wages of corruption. If the Government did really spend money in purchasing votes, it is at least strange, that in these many most secret and confidential communications there is no allusion to, or hint of such proceedings. And it is still stranger, that in the year in which the real contest of the Union was decided, viz., 1799, there was only the small sum of 5,000l. sent over to Lord Castlereagh, the use of which can be, as we shall see, perfectly explained and justified.

The first of the letters of Lord Castlereagh asking for advances from the English Treasury is dated the 2nd of January, 1799. In this letter he asks for a sum of 5000*l*., which was granted. The writer mentions the use to which he intended to apply the money, viz., the publication of pamphlets and writings recommending a Union. "Already we feel the want, and indeed the absolute necessity of the *primum mobile*. We cannot give that activity to the press which is requisite. We have good materials amongst the young barristers, but we cannot expect them to waste their time and starve into the bargain." He then goes on to apologise for asking this sum, small as it is, as he says he knows the difficulties of the Treasury. Lord Cornwallis tells us "that every publication of merit has been systematically and most extensively circulated,"[1] and we know from other sources that ten thousand copies of Pitt's speech on the Irish Union were published and diffused through the country. This sum of 5000*l*. was the only money sent to Lord Castlereagh in 1799.

It may indeed be said that the publication of pamphlets and speeches recommending a Government measure was a species of bribery. But if this be urged, it is hard to understand the meaning of the expression. It might naturally be thought that laying before the public a full and fair exposition of its policy, and thus explaining it at length to the constituencies, was the most justifiable means to which a constitutional Government could resort.

On the 17th of December, 1799, Lord Castlereagh

[1] *Corn. Corr.* iii. 105.

again asks for an advance in a letter to the Duke of Portland. "Your Grace, I trust, will not be surprised at my requesting that you will assist us in the *same way* and to the *same extent* as you did previous to Mr. Elliot's leaving London. The advantages have been important, and it is very desirable that this request should be complied with without delay." That is, he asks for a further sum of 5,000*l*. No answer was given to this request. On the 2nd of January, 1800, he writes, not to the Duke, but to Mr. King, the Under-Secretary of State : " I am impatient to hear from you on the subject of my letter to the Duke. We are in great distress, and I wish the transmiss was more considerable than the last ; it is very important that we should not be destitute of the means on which so much depends." This request was complied with, though the exact sum sent is not mentioned, for we have a memorandum in King's writing respecting this advance. "It was sent this day to Lord Castlereagh. I ventured so far as to observe to Lord Castlereagh that the fund was good security for a still further sum, though not immediately, if it could be well laid out and furnished on the spot. I trust I did not go too far." The words in King's memorandum, " If it could be well laid out and furnished on the spot," are remarkable. They cannot be referred to money payments for votes. Suspicion itself could hardly extract any meaning from them as applied to such an application of the advance. The words, too, of Lord Castlereagh, " We are in great distress" for the want of such a sum as 5,000*l*., add to our difficulty, if we suppose that this small advance was intended for the purchase of votes. Unless we are determined to guide our judgment by what Carlyle calls "preternatural suspicion," we may dismiss these two letters of Lord Castlereagh from any further consideration.

The next letter is the only one which affords any ground for doubt. We shall first give it, and the answer from England, as abstracted in the Cornwallis correspondence, for they are not given in full. We shall then set out the letter in full, and the answer also in full, so far as it relates to Lord Castlereagh's application. Our readers will remark a few mistakes in the letter, and serious changes in the answer which alter its character materially.

The Cornwallis abstract of Lord Castlereagh's letter runs as follows:—

"VISCOUNT CASTLEREAGH to JOHN KING, ESQ.

"Private and Secret.

"DUBLIN CASTLE, *Feb.* 27*th*, 1800.

"MY DEAR SIR,—

". . . . I see no prospect of converts; the Opposition are steady to each other. I hope we shall be able to keep our friends true. A few votes[1] might have a very injurious effect. We require *your assistance*, and you *must* be prepared to enable us to fulfil the expectations which it was impossible to avoid creating at the moment of difficulty. You may be sure[2] we have rather erred on the side of moderation. . . ."

Lord Castlereagh appears to have been "in great distress" at this time, for two days later, on the 1st of March, 1800, the Irish Under-Secretary, Mr. Cooke, writes

[1] This word "votes" should be "rats." See the letter in full, *post.*
[2] "Sure" should be "assured."

to hasten the transmission of the money, and it would seem that he was obliged to go to London about it, for it is from him that the answer comes. It is abstracted thus in the Cornwallis correspondence :—

"EDWARD COOKE to VISCOUNT CASTLEREAGH.
" Secret.
"LONDON, *April* 5*th*, 1800.
"MY DEAR LORD,—
"I have seen the Duke of Portland and Mr. Pitt a second time. The Duke is anxious to send you the needful. Mr. Pitt was equally disposed, but fears it is impossible to the extent. He will continue [1] to let you have from 8,000*l*. to 10,000*l*. for five years.[2] I hope to find out to-night what sum can be sent."[3]

Here is Lord Castlereagh's letter in full :—[4]

" DUBLIN CASTLE, *Feb.* 27*th*, 1800.
" MY DEAR SIR,—
" We were disappointed to-day in our attendance. To-morrow we go on with commerce. Several evidences are summon'd, which will delay us. We shall sit every day, and tire them out if they attempt to make a vexatious delay.
"I see no prospect of converts. The Opposition are steady to each other. I hope we shall be able to keep our friends true. A few rats might have a very injurious effect. We require *your assistance*, and you *must be* prepared to enable us to fulfil the expectations which it was impossible to avoid creating at the moment of difficulty. You may be assured we have rather err'd on the side of moderation.

---

[1] This word "continue" is a mistake for "contrive."
[2] Three sentences are here left out.
[3] The rest of the abstract refers to other matters. The whole letter is very imperfectly abstracted. See letter in full, *post*.
[4] Received from the Public Records Office, London. The writer gratefully acknowledges the courtesy and promptitude with which his requests for information were met in the Record Offices in London and Dublin.

"The prices of subsistence here are very extravagant. We have instituted a committee to inquire into our prospects. We are tolerably well provided in oats and potatoes; wheat and barley certainly deficient, the supply coastways being interrupted by the prevalence of easterly winds. The northern counties have been much embarrassed."

The Treasury was in no hurry to reply to this demand. The answer in full, as far as it relates to Lord Castlereagh's request, runs as follows :—[1]

"MR. COOKE to LORD CASTLEREAGH.
"Secret.
"LONDON, *April 5th*, 1800.

" MY DEAR LORD,—
"I have seen the Duke of Portland and Mr. Pitt a second time. The Duke is anxious to send you the needful. Mr. Pitt was equally disposed, but fears it is impossible to the extent. He will contrive to let you have from 8,000*l*. to 10,000*l*. for five years. He will make no alterations. However, the woollen manufacturers press that, as the raw material is to be given, all the duties on woollens should cease. Mr. Pitt wishes you could let him know the sense of the Irish manufacturers on this point, in case they should wish the abolition of duties. He will, however, keep things as they are; but doing so may occasion delay. I hope to find out to-night what sum can be sent."

We have here a clear request from Lord Castlereagh to the Treasury for money to enable him to satisfy expectations created "at the moment of difficulty." To whom was the money to be given? The prejudiced and partial, who conclude without inquiring, affect to believe that it was intended to be given to Irish members of Parliament for having relieved by their votes the

[1] The whole letter is given in the *Cast. Corr.* iii. 260.

Government in a moment of difficulty, but to this solution there are objections so grave as to be insurmountable.

1. If it was to be given to members for their votes, the moment of difficulty must have occurred in Parliament. But when could this difficulty have arisen? It must have happened, if at all, either in the session of 1799 or that of 1800. At the time Lord Castlereagh's application was written, more than a twelvemonth had passed since the slightest difficulty had arisen in Parliament. Nine months, all but two days, had elapsed since the Parliament had risen on the 1st of June, 1799. How are we to account for the silence of Lord Castlereagh during these nine months, and his long delay in applying for the means of rewarding those who had helped him in his moment of difficulty?

The moment of difficulty could hardly have happened in the session of 1800. The Parliament met on the 15th of January. On the very first night the Government had a majority of forty-two; on the 5th of February, a majority of forty-three; and on the 18th of February, nine days before Lord Castlereagh's letter was written, a majority of forty-six. On the 24th of February, three days before the letter was written, the seventh article of the Union, out of eight in all propounded by Lord Castlereagh, was carried without a division, after a motion that the Speaker should leave the chair had been defeated by a majority of forty-two. The Government had been for more than a year, and was then, so prosperous in all their proceedings in Parliament, that it would have been pure wantonness on their part to have risked their credit in buying votes in face of an Opposition on the look out for accusations against them, and who were nightly declaiming on the corruption of Government.

2. What are we to think of the insignificance of the sum promised, "from 8,000*l*. to 10,000*l*. for five years"? What would have been the use of such a sum when the Opposition at this very time were boasting that they had 100,000*l*. collected, and were offering 5,000*l*. ready money for a vote? On the 29th of January, 1800, Lord Castlereagh writes to the Duke of Portland: "We have undoubted proofs, though not such as we can disclose, that they are enabled to offer as high as 5,000*l*. for an individual vote." On the 8th of February, 1800, Lord Cornwallis states: "The enemy, to my certain knowledge, offer 5,000*l*. ready money for a vote." These statements are not the unsupported allegations of political opponents; they are substantiated by what we have seen is acknowledged in *Grattan's Life* and in Barrington's writings. It is beyond doubt that Whaley received 4,000*l*. from the Opposition to change sides and vote against the Union in the month of February, 1800.

3. If this promised money was to be spent in rewarding those who had voted for the Government, how are we to account for the transitory duration of the reward? Why should the recompense of a needy member be limited to five years? This is inexplicable. Such a person would know that his vote would help to extinguish the assembly which offered him an opportunity of future profits. As its extinction would be perpetual, he would naturally expect a provision for life, or such a sum down as would compensate him for closing for ever

the sources of his emoluments. If any of the Irish members sold their votes for a share in a small annual sum for five years, they were certainly content with a low price and a very imperfect security. If corruption was so rife at this period, as has been alleged, how much more secure it would have been to have obtained a place or a pension, or at least the promise of such, since according to this theory they were content with the promise of payment.

4. The money was not sent at once; there was merely a promise of an annual sum for five years. Great Britain is not usually so niggard in her rewards for services rendered, or in her expenditure to facilitate a political change. A single payment, at the time of the Union with Scotland, to smooth difficulties and to keep the Scotch merchants quiet, cost England nearly 400,000*l*.[1] To incorporate the Isle of Man with her customs' system, Great Britain was content to expend half a million.[2] Yet on the occasion of which we are speaking, it is evident from Pitt's answer that the demand of Lord Castlereagh was unexpected, and that the advance of the money was attended with difficulty; "he will contrive to let you have from 8,000*l*. to 10,000*l*. for five years." On the other hand, there was no hesitation on the part of the Irish members to accept the promise of Lord Castlereagh, rather than the ready money of the Opposition. It is a demand upon our credulity to believe that these traitors were satisfied with the promise

---

[1] The "equivalent," as it was called, amounted to 398,085*l*. 10*s*.
[2] 430,000*l*. in 1826. 70,000*l*. and a pension of 2,000*l*. a year had been given previously.

of a share in 8,000*l.* or 10,000*l.* for five years when they had only to walk across the floor of the House to receive each his 5,000*l.* ready money for recording his vote for the continuance of a Parliament to which he owed his influence and importance. If these Irish members were not honest, and the accusation declares they were not, they were at least possessed of moderation in the highest degree. For as they were to be satisfied with a share in " from 8,000*l.* to 10,000*l.* for five years " they could not have made a very hard bargain with the Government for their votes, and that, too, in a moment of difficulty.

We have suggested reasons which make it improbable that the "moment of difficulty" alluded to by Lord Castlereagh, could have occurred in Parliament, or that his letter referred to members of that assembly. Were there no bodies or classes out of Parliament which might have created a difficulty or delayed the passing of the Union ? Were the manufacturers of Ireland likely to remain quiet and silent when it was proposed to abolish the protective duties which enabled them to exist in the face of English competition, and when there was a compact Opposition in Parliament ready to seize on every opportunity which might occasion embarrassment to the Government or delay in the measure of Union ?[1] A short time before the 27th of February, a "moment of

[1] The aim of the anti-Unionists at this time, as Plunket said in the House, was "to defeat the measure, to decline any responsibility, to avoid giving it any sanction, to leave it encumbered with all its imperfections, that the public might be convinced of its ruinous tendency, and join in reprobating it."—Cornwallis to Portland, 25th Feb. 1800.

difficulty," outside of Parliament, had arrived to Lord Castlereagh, and at the time he was writing the letter of that date, the anti-Unionists, who had seized on the opportunity, were making use of it to alarm the mercantile interests and to excite an uproar against the Union. Our readers will have remarked the abrupt appearance of Lord Castlereagh's demand for an advance in a letter otherwise purely commercial, and the still more abrupt appearance of Pitt's promise among matters referring to the alteration of duties. The sudden transition from Pitt's promise, " he will contrive to let you have from 8000*l.* to 10,000*l.* for five years," to the words, " he will make no alterations : however the woollen manufacturers press that, &c.," shows us that the mind of the writer was not dwelling on matters of bribery, but on the proposed changes in the tariff. A consideration of the context of the answer, and a knowledge of what was then going on before a committee of the Irish Commons will suggest that this annual sum for five years was not intended for members of Parliament at all, but was to be distributed among some Irish manufacturers who were likely to suffer from the new duties between the two countries.

The sixth article of the Union, that is, the commercial one, had been carried on the 21st of February, and a committee of the House was engaged in taking evidence, as is referred to in Lord Castlereagh's letter,[1] as to the way in which the Irish manufacturers would be affected by the duties proposed to be inserted in the schedule attached to the article. Before the Union the

[1] " To-morrow we go on with commerce," etc.

Irish manufacturers of cotton and muslin were protected by prohibitory duties varying from 35 to 50 per cent.,[1] and the English manufacturers were able to undersell the Irish by the latter amount.[2] It was proposed by Pitt at first to equalise the duties between the two countries, and for this purpose to reduce, among others, those on calicoes and muslins at once to 10 per cent. The Irish manufacturers petitioned against the reduction, produced evidence and were heard by counsel before a committee of the House. Lord Castlereagh thought that this class had made out a case of hardship, and was at this time pressing Pitt to consent to a postponement of the reduction of the duties. The Irish trade in calicoes and muslins was an important one, and gave employment to between 30,000 and 40,000 hands.[3] Pitt was very unwilling to consent to any postponement, as, to use his own words, it would interfere with the "general principle of liberal intercourse which we wish to establish." Besides, he was importuned by the English manufacturers that as the raw material would go free to Ireland, all the protective duties should cease.

[1] "But of all the articles the one that affects us most is *cotton*. By the petition presented a few hours ago, it appears that the present duties on plain calicoes may be estimated at between 40 and 50 per cent. of the value ; on plain muslins about 35 per cent. ; and on coloured, or worked, or figured, very little less."— Speech of Right Hon. J. Foster, 17th Feb. 1800. *Cast. Corr.* iii. 205.

[2] This was given in evidence by the Irish manufacturers.—*Ib.*

[3] "It is evident . . . that a sudden reduction of the duty must, at least for a time, ruin the trade which now employs from 30,000 to 40,000 persons. The individuals have little capital to bear a shock." —Castlereagh to Rose, 7th March, 1800. *Cast. Corr.* iii. 251.

While the Irish manufacturers were pressing their complaints respecting the reduction of the duties, and the danger to their trade, the anti-Unionists saw their opportunity, and did not let it slip. Their language aroused a strong feeling among the manufacturing and commercial interests.[1] Both Lord Cornwallis and Lord Castlereagh "were very anxious to conciliate these classes, whose influence lay principally in the north of Ireland, where the mass of the population was at this time perfectly loyal."[2] Lord Castlereagh resolved to deprive the anti-Unionists of the means of exciting the country, and raising a cry against the Union. He therefore proposed to the manufacturers a compromise, viz., that these duties should be continued for five years. Pitt consented to this, lest, as he tells Lord Castlereagh, "you should expose yourself to any risk, or even any material additional difficulty in the general system."[3] The Irish manufacturers held out for a further extension of time, and Lord Castlereagh, who had obtained from Pitt permission to use his own discretion,[4] was so anxious to cut the ground from under the anti-Unionists, that he consented to a prolongation for seven instead of five years. It is possible, even probable, when we consider the wording of Pitt's answer to Lord Castlereagh's request for an advance, that the sum of "from 8,000*l.* to 10,000*l.* for five years" was a portion of the terms given to the Irish manufacturers to keep them quiet, and induce them to accept the compromise offered by Lord Castlereagh. This is

[1] *Corn. Corr.* iii. 217.
[2] *Ib.*
[3] *Cast. Corr.* iii. 250.
[4] *Ib.* 251.

rendered even more probable by the fact that some time previously Lord Castlereagh had it under his consideration to compensate the Irish cotton manufacturers by the payment of the large sum of 200,000*l.*[1]

On the hypothesis of the bribery of members of Parliament, we might naturally expect that the passing of the Union Bill would put an end to any further demands. But we shall find that they go on to the 5th of May, 1801, eleven months after the Bill had been carried in the Commons, by a majority of sixty-five. On the 10th of July, 1800, Mr. Marsden writes to Cooke, who must have been in London : " Lord Castlereagh wishes me to remind you of the necessity of supplies; we are in great want." And on the 12th Lord Castlereagh also writes to the same gentleman: " I hope you will settle with King our further ways and means ; from the best calculation I can make we shall *absolutely* require the remainder of what I asked for, namely fifteen, to wind up matters, exclusive of the annual arrangement, and an immediate supply is much wanted ; if it cannot be sent speedily, I hope we may discount it here. Pray arrange this, and if they could give General Budé[2] his 300*l.* in England, it would be very convenient at this moment of extreme pressure."

No attention appears to have been paid to this request, for five months later, on the 9th of December, 1800, Mr. Cooke (Lord Castlereagh being then absent)

---

[1] *Cast. Corr.* iii. 207.
[2] A French emigrant. Lord Castlereagh's request was not attended to. General Budé's pension was charged on the Irish establishment.

writes to Mr. King : "There are several matters which have been recently officially recommended by the Lord-Lieutenant, and as the time of the Union approaches, it is extremely wished that every matter depending should be concluded before that time."

Upon this letter Mr. King writes the significant memorandum: "I know of none except the arrangements of the Secretary's office and the Catholic question, to which no answer has been given, and even with respect to those they have been told that they could not be determined till Lord Castlereagh should arrive."

On the same day on which Cooke wrote to King, viz., the 9th of December, Mr. Marsden also writes to him : "I am induced to write to you from the great degree of inconvenience which I am subjected to, by the delay in sending over the King's letter for putting into our hands the money saved in the Civil List in this country, to be applied to secret service here. It has fallen to my lot to make a considerable number of engagements, which this money was to discharge, and I am pressed, in some instances in the most inconvenient degree, to make good my promises."

No answer was given to this pressing demand, for Mr. Marsden again writes to King, on the 6th of May, 1801 : "I am again under the necessity of entreating your aid to have our money matters settled. I have already informed you how distressingly I am, more than any one, embarked in this business, and since I wrote to you nothing has been received." This is the last letter on the subject.

In examining the facts of history, we ought not to

give undue predominance to suspicion, or allow it to
press upon our judgment. Is it not absurd to refer
every act of the Government to the worst motives, when
we know that there were many ways in which these
two small sums of "from 8,000*l.* to 10,000*l.* for five
years" and 15,000*l.* might have have been properly and
justly expended? The Government must have entered
into innumerable engagements during the rebellion and
the disturbed times which succeeded it. Up to July,
1800, "the most strenuous exertions of the military
had failed to extirpate the banditti who infested some
of the wild and mountainous parts of Ireland."[1] In
1799 and 1800, Ireland was in a lamentable condition,[2]
and still seething in disaffection which was kept alive
up to Emmett's rebellion in 1803. Spies had to be

[1] *Corn. Corr.* iii. 282.

[2] The correspondence of Lord Cornwallis presents a terrible picture
of the country. These are some extracts :—" From the most authentic
channels we learn that the disaffected are more active than ever in
swearing and organising the southern provinces."—28th Jan. 1799.
"The mails and travellers are frequently intercepted and robbed, the
roads being infested with banditti. The centres of Wicklow and
Wexford remain disturbed.... and in the West the old system of
houghing cattle has been of late revived and carried to an extent
which threatens the most serious consequences, not only to this
kingdom, but to the Empire."—14th Feb. "Robberies and murders
continue frequent in various parts, and there is every symptom that
the mind of the lower classes is in general much agitated and preparing for new mischief."—23rd Feb. "The state of the kingdom
is such, from the extended nature of the conspiracy, that acts of
rebellion are breaking out from time to time in almost every part."—
12th March. "The county of Waterford and a part of Cork and
Tipperary are in an unpleasant state; meetings are held, and illegal
oaths tendered, and the disaffected are very busy working mischief."
—24th Oct.

paid, informers to be maintained, past services to be remunerated, and rewards for apprehensions to be offered. For example, in July, 1800, a reward of 210*l.* was offered in a proclamation for the capture of each of the first ten robbers named on a list, or of 2,100*l.* in a single matter.[1] If we consider, or are able to conceive the numerous and multifarious engagements of this kind and others, which the Government must have entered into for the protection of the country, and if we keep in mind the total change about to be effected, we shall deem the demands on the Treasury during the year 1800, viz., the two sums of "8,000*l.* or 10,000*l.* for five years," and 15,000*l.*, not only not extravagant, but entirely disproportionate to the necessities of the times.

The accusation of corruption was grappled with by the Government and its supporters in both Houses of Parliament, and the Opposition was challenged to prove it. In the House of Lords, the Chancellor, Lord Clare, on the 10th of February, 1800, accused the anti-Unionists of having opened an exchequer "for foul and undisguised bribery," and named two members who were present in connection with his allegation. These peers attempted to defend themselves, but no counter-charge was brought forward. It is incredible, that if the Government had not been conscious of the integrity of their intentions, they would have allowed their Chancellor to dare the Opposition to the proof, or that that body, thus challenged, would have refrained from attempting to prove their case against the Government.

[1] *Corn. Corr.* iii. 282.

In the Commons, the highest officer of the law, the Prime Sergeant, who took rank before the Attorney-General, on the 15th of January, 1800, thus threw down the glove. "Some persons had had the temerity (for in their situation he could call it by no other name) to charge His Majesty's Government with corruption in carrying forward the measure of a Union. He should beg leave to contrast the conduct of that Government with the conduct of those who had ventured to bring forward that charge, some of whom had talked that night of proving facts at the bar; that, it was well known, was a stage-trick to catch the mob; they were dared, they were challenged to do so. The same trick was practised last session by a learned gentleman (Mr. M.) who chose to make himself the little hero of the story, but when he was pressed to come forward, the learned member shrunk from his own calumny."[1] In the preceding year also, this gentleman had challenged the Opposition to prove their accusation of bribery. On that occasion he ended his speech with these words: "It was base to be bribed, very base, but it was baser to make the charge when it was known to be false."[2] The glove thus thrown down was not taken up in either House. The accusation was allowed to remain then, as it has ever since continued, a subject for declamation, but not a matter for serious proof.

It must be distinctly understood that the particular accusation we are now investigating, namely, that money was given by the Government to members for

[1] *Parl. Reg.* J. Milliken, Dublin, 1800.
[2] *Parl. Deb.* J. Moore, Dublin, 1799.

their votes, was never made in the Irish Parliament. This charge is a growth of later times, and is founded, if such a word can be applied to it, upon the letters we have been considering. The accusations of the Opposition at the time of the Union were vague and general, and were based upon three circumstances: the compensation for boroughs; the dismissal of officers and the promotions consequent on their dismissals; and the alleged terms offered to the Protestant, Catholic, and Presbyterian Churches. Plunket and Grattan were the principal members of the Opposition who urged the charge of corruption. Their statements may excite our admiration of their oratorical powers, but they are very far from establishing their case. " During the interval," says Plunket, " between the sessions [of 1799 and 1800], the same barefaced system of parliamentary corruption has been pursued—dismissals, promotions, threats, promises .... bribes were promised to the Catholic clergy; bribes were promised to the Presbyterian clergy .... and to crown all, you openly avow that the constitution of Ireland is to be purchased for a stipulated sum. I state it as a fact, that you cannot dare to deny, that 15,000*l.* apiece is to be given to certain individuals as the price for surrendering what? their property? No! but the right of representation of the people of Ireland." And on the same occasion Grattan said, "We will now come to the bribes he [Pitt] holds out. And first he begins with the Church. To the Protestant Church he promises perpetual security; to the Catholic Church his advocates promise eventual salary, and both hold out to the farmer commutation of tithes . . . . the minister proceeds, he proposes his third bribe, namely, the abolition of tithes . . . . the minister has not done with bribes; whatever economy he shows in argument, here he has been generous in the extreme. Parson, priest, I think one of his advocates hints the Presbyterians, not forgotten, and now the mercantile body are all to be bribed that all may be ruined. He holds out commercial benefits for political annihilation."[1] It is in such vague and general declamation as this, that we find the germs from which the accusations of corruption and bribery against the Government and the Unionists have ripened. It is a melancholy reflection that there are sensible and intelligent men who regard the rhetorical exaggerations and misrepresentations of Plunket and Grattan as facts and proofs.

Finally, is no regard to be paid to the character of Lord Cornwallis, and to his distinct denial that bribery was resorted to? Is the testimony of one who lived a life of honour, valour, and patriotism, to weigh nothing against mere suspicion? After his services in Ireland, Lord Cornwallis went to India a second time, well knowing that he did so at the risk of his life,[2] and died there, a sacrifice, if ever there was one, to the call of duty. The breath of slander has never ventured to sully his name. The Governor who purified the services in India was not likely to dabble in corruption in

---

[1] For Plunket's and Grattan's speeches see *Parl. Reg.*, Milliken, Dublin, 1800, pp. 99 and 130-1.

[2] "It is a desperate act to embark for India at the age of sixty-six."—Lord Cornwallis to General Ross, 24th Oct., 1804.

Ireland, and the choice of such a man by the Government to carry the Union, ought to be a guarantee to us, that they were resolved to pass that measure by honest and constitutional means.

Perhaps there never was a man less fitted for intrigue and corruption than Lord Cornwallis. On the occasion of every national crisis there are men to be found whose only desire is, to turn it to their own advantage, and to extract from the public necessity private gains. In his position, Lord Cornwallis was obliged to listen to the offers of such men, and to hear the demands made for their undesirable co-operation. It was his duty to conciliate the wavering and the timid, and to avoid changing into irreconcilable enemies the self-seeking trimmers whom such a time brings forth. We know the disgust which his interviews with these jobbers caused him. To the sympathetic ear of his friend General Ross he confides his feelings. "The political jobbing of this country gets the better of me; it has ever been the wish of my life to avoid all this dirty business, and I am now involved in it beyond all bearing, and am consequently more wretched than ever. . . . . How I long to kick those whom my public duty obliges me to court. . . . . The leaders of the Opposition, who know and eagerly pursue their own little dirty interests, although they are so blind as not to see that they must be overwhelmed in the general wreck, have art enough to instil their own narrow and wicked sentiments into the thoughtless though selfish members, and in the hopes of getting 300*l.* or 400*l.* a year at a distant period, they will hazard as many thousands which they at present possess."[1] Yet, while he expresses his horror of political jobbers, he never loses an opportunity of loyally praising his ministers and the members of his own party. His letters are full of cordial commendations of Lords Castlereagh and Clare, and of the subordinates who supported his policy in Parliament and in the country. Lord Cornwallis was not one of those leaders who attribute all the glory of a contest to themselves; he was ever ready to share the credit with the followers who bore a part in the fray. And his approval is a proof to us that he did not believe that those subordinates were engaged in schemes of bribery and corruption.

It has been charged against the Government that they poured enormous numbers of troops into Ireland for the purpose of over-awing the people and carrying the Union by intimidation. This accusation is unfounded, and may be dismissed with a few words. Considering the state of the country and the threatening attitude of the French, the forces in Ireland, far from being numerous, were inadequate. We have a return, made by Lord Cornwallis on the 19th July, 1799, of the whole available force in the country. A rebellion which had assumed the character of a war of extermination had just been put down, two French invasions had lately taken place, and Ireland was frightfully disturbed. In March 1799, a large French fleet was assembled in the Texel, and another at Brest. It was believed in England that both were intended for Ireland, for when a gale of wind forced Lord Bridport, the British Admiral,

[1] *Corn. Corr.* iii. 101.

to raise the blockade, he sailed at once for Ireland where he expected to find the French fleet. Yet at this time of danger there were but 45,419 regular soldiers in Ireland, besides artillery. Several of the fencible regiments, were in an inefficient condition, and Lord Cornwallis was of opinion that no reliance could be placed on the Irish Militia, as indeed the rout at Castlebar had shown. On the 24th July, 1799, Lord Cornwallis wrote to the Duke of Portland in these words: "The force remaining in Ireland is sufficient to preserve peace, totally inadequate to repel foreign invasion."[1] This letter was written twelve months before the passing of the Act of Union, and in the very middle of the political struggle.

[1] *Corn. Corr.* iii. 118.

THE END.

www.ingramcontent.com/pod-product-compliance
Lightning Source LLC
Chambersburg PA
CBHW031740230426
43669CB00007B/421